ESSAYS AND STUDIES
1979

ESSAYS AND STUDIES
1979

BEING VOLUME THIRTY-TWO OF THE NEW SERIES
OF ESSAYS AND STUDIES COLLECTED FOR
THE ENGLISH ASSOCIATION

BY DIETER MEHL

JOHN MURRAY

FIFTY ALBEMARLE STREET LONDON

Set, printed and bound in Great Britain by
Cox & Wyman Ltd, London, Fakenham and Reading

0 7195 3636 7

Contents

The Relationship between the Hengwrt and the Ellesmere Manuscripts of the 'Canterbury Tales'

N. F. BLAKE

THOSE who have written on the order of the tales in the *Canterbury Tales* have worked on the assumption that Chaucer had some plan to which he was working. Thus the decision in Pro[1] that each pilgrim was to tell two tales on the journey out and another two on the journey home might provide the basis of his original plan. Hence there has been a concerted effort to discover how the extant tales fit into this scheme by recourse to the following types of information: the names of places such as Deptford mentioned in the links; the dates and times of day, as at $B^1$5-14 where it is said to be 10 a.m. on 18 April; and verbal echoes between passages.[2] The presupposition is that the final order must be realistic geographically and chronologically, although it is recognized that there are inconsistencies which cannot be ironed out however much the tales are rearranged.[3]

The attempt to find the right order has centred round the testimony of El. Some scholars, like Skeat, consider it an edited text, while others, like Brusendorff, think it most faithfully preserves Chaucer's intentions.[4] Most modern scholars seem to be closer to

[1] I use the abbreviations of manuscripts and tales found in J. M. Manly and E. Rickert, *The Text of the Canterbury Tales*, 8 vols (Chicago, 1940): see I. xix–xxiii.

[2] For the significance read into the echo between E1212 and E1213 see R. A. Pratt, *The Tales of Canterbury* (Boston, 1974), p. 342. See also R. F. Jones, 'A Conjecture on the Wife of Bath's Prologue', *JEGP*, 24 (1925), 521–32.

[3] Cf. the comment in J. S. P. Tatlock, 'The *Canterbury Tales* in 1400', *PMLA*, 50 (1935), 127: 'The nearly fixed and consistent order which was elicited long ago, perhaps confirmed here, almost the only such order possible, is found in not a single text out of the fifty-seven'.

[4] W. W. Skeat, *The Evolution of the Canterbury Tales* (London: Chaucer Society, 2nd ser 38, 1907), p. 22; A Brusendorff, *The Chaucer Tradition* (Oxford, 1925), pp. 106–7.

Brusendorff on this point, since all editions are to a greater or lesser extent based on El's order. But recently there has arisen the feeling, partly because of Manly's work though it was not his opinion, that the best text is that found in Hg. This has produced the unhappy result that editions follow Hg textually but El in tale order.[1] But if El has the best order, why does it not have the best text; and likewise if Hg has the best text, why does it not have the best order? The answer is partly historical. Early editors followed El in both text and tale order, for the preference for Hg's text is relatively new and even now not universal. But all critical scholarship, particularly that dealing with structure, has necessarily proceeded on the basis that El's order is correct since all editions use it. As Hg's order differs considerably from El's, it is dismissed as disordered.

The problem of tale order is complicated by our inability to decide in what state the poem existed at Chaucer's death. Manly took the view that individual tales and groups circulated privately in Chaucer's lifetime and that they were copied possibly without his permission or knowledge. He arrived at this conclusion partly because in his opinion the individual tales had varying textual traditions and partly because of the way Hg was put together. Furthermore the *Lenvoy de Chaucer a Bukton* which mentions the wife of Bath presupposes that some friends at least knew something of the *Canterbury Tales*. Tatlock, on the other hand, favoured the idea that there was little circulation before 1400 and that the scribes put together the material they found in Chaucer's study.[2] That this view has much to be said for it was indicated by a series of articles by Mrs Dempster.[3] She showed that the later manuscript groups depend upon the earlier ones and that *c* (the earliest

[1] This is most strikingly seen in the work of E. T. Donaldson. He used Hg as his base text in his *Chaucer's Poetry*, 2nd edn (New York, 1975), p. v. But he has argued for the order of El in 'The Ordering of the *Canterbury Tales*', *Medieval Literature and Folklore Studies: Essays in Honor of F. L. Utley* (ed. J. Mandel and B. Rosenberg, New Brunswick, N. J., 1970), pp. 193–204.

[2] G. Dempster, 'Manly's Conception of the Early History of the *Canterbury Tales*', *PMLA*, 61 (1946), 379–415 and Tatlock *art. cit.*, 100–39.

[3] 'A Chapter in the Manuscript History of the *Canterbury Tales*', *PMLA*, 63 (1948), 456–84, and 'The Fifteenth-Century Editors of the *Canterbury Tales* and the Problem of Tale Order', *PMLA*, 64 (1949), 1123–42.

of these later groups) is based on Hg and group *a* with which El is closely linked. Since she also realized that El might be descended from Hg, the possibility was there that most, if not all, manuscripts descend ultimately from one source. While this would not disprove the concept of prior circulation, it would mean it had no support in the manuscript tradition.

Clearly the position of Hg is crucial in the history of the manuscripts. In this article I shall first examine how Hg was put together in an attempt to show that its composition proves it is the earliest extant manuscript. I shall go on to examine El to show that its order can be understood only as a development of Hg's order. I shall try to avoid the trap of accepting pieces as genuine because I like them or because they have always been part of the canon; the manuscripts must be allowed to speak for themselves. As far as Hg is concerned I make the assumption that the scribe or editor had all the fragments before he started; I do not think he acquired them piecemeal. It is agreed that Chaucer was still working on the poem when he died. Even if he had published some tales, we must accept that he kept a copy of each tale (in its revised form if it had been revised). Not to do so would imply that he did not consider the fragments part of one poem which he hoped to finish and publish eventually in its entirety. There was a complete set of fragments among his papers when he died. Since the earliest manuscripts are dated to the first decade of the fifteenth century, publication of the poem was set in hand shortly, if not immediately, after his death. If the scribe of Hg acquired the fragments piecemeal, he did not have them all when he started copying. This was what led Manly to propose the theory of prior circulation. But why should an editor acquire fragments of the poem from different courtly readers when he knew perfectly well that a complete set of fragments was surely to be found in Chaucer's house? We have no right to assume the editor was so foolish. Alternatively we have to accept that on Chaucer's death his set was dispersed and then within a few years, or even months, attempts were made to reassemble the fragments. That would be a desperate solution. Furthermore, if there was an 'editorial office' issuing different fragments to various scribes, that office would have access to all the fragments and so be able to advise the scribes about order. The most natural hypothesis is that on Chaucer's death his 'literary executors' found his set of fragments and one of them acting as editor employed the scribe of Hg to make the first 'complete' copy of the poem. Convincing arguments need to be adduced to negate this expectation.

Manly thought he had found such an argument in the different inks in Hg.[1] He identified three: a dark brown for most of the manuscript, a light brown for D, and a yellowish for the end of B² (from MkT–NPT link onwards) with all H and a few insertions (F673–708, 709–20). These inks represented to him three different periods of copying. The bulk of the manuscript in dark brown ink was written first, then D, and finally the pieces in yellowish ink. But at least some of what is in the yellow ink appears to have been available to the scribe when he was writing in the dark brown ink. Only a part of the prologue to FkT is in yellow ink (709–20), the rest is in dark brown (721–8). It is almost certain, as argued below, that the scribe had F709–20 when he copied the later part. Consequently if the inks do represent three stages in copying, it need not follow that the scribe did not have all the copy before he started work. In any case it is more probable that the part in yellow ink was written immediately after that in dark brown, for it commences with the explicit of MkT and thus carries straight on from what precedes in the middle of a constant group. Also it is not necessary to assume, as Manly did, that in writing Hg the scribe began with Pro and copied his material in the order he intended for the poem. If Hg is the earliest manuscript and if the editor had a collection of unordered fragments to arrange, he may have got the scribe to copy A and I first, because as the beginning and end they were fixed points. That he put I last suggests that Rt was in his copytext. When he finalized the order of the intermediate fragments, the scribe would copy them ending up with the section in yellow ink.

What then about D which is written in the light brown ink? It is agreed that D was inserted later between A and MLPT because it interrupts Manly's reconstructed quire sequence. If so,

[1] See Manly-Rickert I. 266–83 and II. 475–9 for a description of Hg.

either the scribe did not have D when he started copying or he meant it to be fitted in elsewhere. As he appears to have had the rest of the poem, the latter is more likely. At this point we may consider the evidence of PsP which at I1 in Hg reads 'By that the maunciple hadde his tale al ended'. The word 'maunciple' is written on an erasure. Tatlock correctly indicated that the size of the erasure meant the only pilgrims who could fit I1 were the prioress, the merchant, the summoner, the pardoner, the plow-man and the carpenter, and that of these the summoner was the most probable.[1] The plowman and the carpenter have no tales; the merchant is not a likely candidate for reasons we shall see; PrT is enclosed inside B[2] and so could not precede I; and although PdT comes at the end of C, in Hg it precedes ShT in the middle of a quire and so cannot have been designed to precede I. The summoner fits the erasure at I1, his tale comes at the end of a group, and that group is not in the position in Hg which it was originally to occupy.[2] I suggest therefore that D was meant to precede I in the original plan. The progress of the manuscript may have been as follows. The scribe copied A first, then I (inserting 'summoner' or 'plowman' at I1) and then proceeded with the intermediate section of the poem from MLPT onwards. Quite fortuitously he started on a yellowish ink with the explicit of MkT. Before he completed McT he decided that it was not appropriate to put D before I. So while filling in some gaps in his yellow ink, he pondered the problem of D. Finally he decided to insert it be-tween A and MLPT, and when he copied it he used a new ink,

---

[1] Tatlock *art. cit.*, 138–9. Manly's suggestion that the original reading was 'Frankeleyn' is improbable.

[2] A possible objection to this is the existence of some marks in Hg which may be part of the original reading. In their introduction to the forthcoming facsimile edition of Hg (Henceforth *Facsimile*) A. I. Doyle and M. B. Parkes suggest that 'Plowman' would fit the marks. If this is correct, I do not think that it would invalidate the possibility of SuT preceding PsT in Hg's original order. It would confirm that I was written after A and before the rest of the poem and suggest that an arbitrary name was inserted at I1 (? because the plowman was the par-son's brother) while the intermediate section was arranged in a sequence. I am indebted to Dr. Doyle and Dr. Parkes for their kindness in letting me see this introduction before it was published, for it has enabled me to make important improvements to my argument.

light brown in colour. The reasons for this change of plan we will consider later.

In their analysis Doyle and Parkes divide Hg into five groups: *I (i.e. A), *II (D), *III (MkPT, NPPT, McPT), *IV (the rest) and *V (I).[1] As they point out *III (which contains the change from brown to yellow ink) should follow *IV and is misbound. As B[2] (a constant group) starts in *IV and finishes in *III, the break between the two is fortuitous; in this instance the beginning of a tale was made to coincide with the quire boundary.[2] The importance of this division is that it supports the view I suggested above that SuT was intended to precede PsPT. For if *II is not in its correct position, the only place available for it is before *V, provided we accept that the scribe had all fragments before he started. Doyle and Parkes, however, do not accept this partly because of the nature of *IV. As it contains two quires of unusual size, an inserted page, varieties in the shading of ink, signs of haste and gaps between tales, they believe the scribe acquired the various parts of *IV at different times, though they do not indicate which parts were acquired together or in what order. These features are rather technical which need not be discussed here (though some are dealt with in footnotes) because their hypothesis may be disproved in a more general way.

*IV is a unit because it represents 'the coincidence of physical and content divisions'. Although it consists of fourteen quires and contains MLPT, SqT, MeT, FkT, SNT, ClT, C and B[2] (as far as TMel), at no point do the boundaries of the tales, let alone the groups, coincide with the quire boundaries. This means that the tales (with the exception of SNT discussed below) were written in the order in which they now occur, for there would be no way of inserting a tale in such a situation. Or rather the insertion of any new material would demand considerable recopying. As the scribe was not prepared to insert D within *IV (where the editor

[1] *Facsimile*. I have added asterisks to the Doyle–Parkes numbers so that their *I (i.e. Group A) should not be confused with I (i.e. their *V).

[2] The reason is probably technical in that *IV finishes with a tale in prose, TMeL. The scribe probably found it more convenient for reasons of ruling not to let the prose tale spill over to the next quire. This apparently affected the quiring of some other *Canterbury Tales* manuscripts.

clearly wanted it to be as we shall see), it is most unlikely that he recopied any other parts. Doyle and Parkes express surprise that the various tales/groups were not written in fascicules since that would allow the scribe to shuffle the parts around after they were written so that he could achieve the best order. Indeed if the various fragments had come to the scribe piecemeal, one would expect him to use that method, a common one at the time. That he did not suggests that he, or the editor, had all the fragments before copying commenced and that he was following a particular plan. The crux of the matter, therefore, is whether the arrangement in Hg, particularly in *IV, exhibits any sign of ordering.

There is a natural break in *IV at SNT, for the arrangement before that tale was MLPT (gap) SqT (gap) MeT (gap)[1] FkT(gap) SNT. In other words the scribe put all the tales which had no preceding (except MLT which is a special case discussed later) or following link in his exemplar into one section, for the succeeding tales are all linked. This alone exhibits a system, which must be attributed to the editor since the likelihood of the linkless tales appearing together by chance is negligible. That this is not the

---

[1] A gap was left at the end of MeT on f.152^v, but this was not subsequently used as a new leaf, f. 153, was inserted in the quire on which was written the MeT–FkT link and that part of the prologue to FkT (F709–20) which was omitted when FkT was copied. It is significant that the omitted section (12 lines) and heading of FkT would fit quite comfortably in the bottom half of f. 152^v which contains the final 18 lines and explicit of MeT. In Hg a folio with two headings contains from 30 to 34 lines of text. It would appear that the scribe was not informed whether there was to be a new link here and so used his initiative by leaving out that piece of FkT which could, if necessary, be inserted later on f. 152^v. When he heard a new link was on its way, he wrote the first twelve lines of FkT on the bottom verso of a loose leaf in the yellow ink. When the link arrived he copied that in a different ink on the recto and top verso of the same leaf and inserted it as f. 153. Since f. 153 had more than enough room to accommodate the new material, he did not need to use f. 152^v. This proposal is adumbrated in Manly-Rickert I. 271–2, but Manly did not realize it invalidated his reasoning that the yellow ink material arrived later. I would go further and say as f. 153 is written in two inks which differ from that used on ff. 152, 154, it indicates the scribe knew a link was coming although it had not arrived when he wrote the part in yellow ink. It is reasonable to interpret this to mean the link was being composed, for how otherwise would he have learned of its existence and likely length and not have it in front of him so that he could copy it at the same time as F709–20?

order we today prefer is unimportant; it is an order. Furthermore if the tales had come to the scribe piecemeal we may wonder why he left gaps between them. He had copied *I and *V and so might assume that there should be links between tales. But after receiving two or three linkless tales, he may well have felt that there were no links in the middle section. It is customary to suggest that he knew there were versions with links available and he was waiting for them to come to hand. This must be the case if, as Doyle and Parkes suggest, *IV was written first. How did he know this? And more importantly, if he did know it he knew more about the poem than the sum of pieces available to him at any time.[1] If this is so the piecemeal theory becomes unnecessary because he could have organized the poem on the basis of that extra knowledge rather than from the pieces he had immediately in front of him. That he should not under these circumstances have used the fascicule method becomes almost incredible.

The other part of *IV contains the linked tales. This too shows an order for the editor arranged the fragments so that every tale was separated from the next by one, and only one, interlude from the pilgrimage frame. ClT opens with an exchange between clerk and host which serves as the link between SNT and ClT. It has the final host stanza which links it with PhT of C. Within C (a constant group) PhT is linked with PdT which ends with the exchange among host, pardoner and knight. This allows ShT which has no linking prologue to follow. Thus B² follows C. B² is a constant group which takes us beyond *IV, but it is worth following the arrangement through to the end of the poem to underline that the editor had a system. In B² there is a constant progression of tale–link–tale from ShT to NPT which in Hg has no endlink. But NPT is linked to McT through McP, the interlude of the drunken cook. McT has no endlink. Originally, as suggested above, D came between H and I. Thus McT was linked to WBT

---

[1] It is unlikely that the scribe knew much about the links until they arrived. In *Facsimile* Doyle and Parkes point out that the gap after MLT was not ruled because the scribe did not know in what metre it was in, for MLT is in stanzas and SqT in couplets. But if he had sufficient knowledge about other versions to know they had links, he would probably have known what metre they were in.

through WBP. D contains the normal tale–link–tale sequence to SuT which has no endlink. But SuT was joined to PsT by PsP. As it happens since D has the same arrangement as H (a link at the beginning but not at the end), the arrangement of tale–link–tale was not disturbed by D's removal.

In other words from SNT to PsT there is a continuous sequence of tale–link–tale (with or without D). This is quite clearly an order which has been contrived by an editor for the chances of that arrangement turning up randomly are negligible. It follows that all fragments were available to the editor before the manuscript was copied so that this order could be imposed upon them. The theory of piecemeal acquisition may be discarded and other reasons will have to be found to account for the manuscript's irregularities.[1] That we have not noticed this order in Hg before arises partly because we are so used to El's order and partly because we want to arrange the tales in a coherent geographical and chronological framework. Any arrangement which fails to meet the latter requirement appears disorganized to us. But we should remember that we have read the poem many times and are familiar with its details. The editor of Hg had perhaps never read the poem before and was evidently in a hurry to publish it. Instead of studying the internal details of the links, he chose the easier course of an order of tale–link–tale—a scheme which existed already in the constant groups. As it happens only a very few modifications are possible if the editor's system is to be kept. Once D is removed, only H could be moved to between SNT and ClT. It is possible to think that H is near the end because of the reference to Bobbe–Up–and–Down in McP. It is impossible to say how far such reasons weighed with the editor who may have been intent on providing a coherent sequence of tale–link–tale, not necessarily the best or only sequence.

As a result of the foregoing discussion we may accept that the editor of Hg had all his copy available before he set the scribe to work. It is reasonable to suppose that his copytext was Chaucer's own set of fragments. The corollary of this is that whatever is not

---

[1] In fact there are few irregularities in quiring in *IV and these are discussed in various footnotes.

in Hg may be considered spurious. The arrangement in Hg indicates that the scribe's copy consisted of the following:

(i) Units consisting of more than one tale or if of one tale only that tale has introduction and/or endlink from the pilgrimage frame: A, I, ClT, C, B^2, H, D.

(ii) Tales with no prologue or endlink from the pilgrimage frame: MLT (B^{1}99–1162), SqT (F9–672), MeT (E1245–2418), FkT (F709–1624), SNT (G1–553).

(iii) Link: MLP (B^1 1–98).

The traditional groups/fragments have no relevance for Hg whose scribe had the above thirteen sections. The sections in (i) need no further discussion, but the others do.

As we saw earlier, when the scribe wrote the tales in (ii) he left gaps between them, two of which were subsequently filled. Why were these gaps left? Manly, pursuing his theory of prior circulation, suggested he did so in the hope that the links would turn up. But even if we could believe in prior circulation (a theory I hope to have shown untenable), the explanation would be inadequate in that it merely pushes the problem one stage further back. Hg's MeT–FkT link, for example, refers specifically to MeT and can have been written only to follow it. Since, as far as we can tell, the links in groups like A always circulated with the tales of their group, it is most unlikely that a link specifically made for a particular tale by Chaucer would have become separated from that tale. For such a theory to be convincing we would need to know why a link like Hg's MeT–FkT link became separated from its tale whereas other links did not.

Two other views are possible. The first is that the links were available but the scribe did not know where they were to be placed. It could be that Chaucer sometimes composed links and tales independently and only married them together later. In that case it could be that he died before uniting the tales with the links. But quite apart from the names of the pilgrims in them, these two links have many features which tie them to the tales they follow. The endlink of MeT refers unequivocally to a bad wife (E2420) and so can refer only to MeT of these five tales. The endlink to SqT refers to the speaker's youth, and a comparison is made between his virtuous excellence and the dissolute behaviour of the next speaker's son. It is difficult to think that this endlink would fit any of the other tales. Consequently this view is unacceptable.

The second possibility is that the links were not available because they had not yet been written, for they were written later to fill the gaps. We saw in the last paragraph how closely these links are tied to the tales they follow. Their specific nature is what one might expect from someone who was trying to complete gaps left at particular places. Indeed the editor might have told the scribe to put these tales first in the middle section of the poem so that he could have time to get the appropriate links written. He would simply instruct the scribe to leave a gap, usually to the end of the folio in question, after each tale.

Two important points arise from a recognition that the links (E2419–40 with F1–8, and F673–708) are spurious. The first is that these tales were in progress at Chaucer's death and not yet incorporated into the framework of the poem, though presumably intended to be so included. Thus SqT is incomplete in a different way from MkT or TTh. The latter two were meant to be incomplete for dramatic reasons within the linking frame; SqT was incomplete because Chaucer had not finished it. Similarly the gaps in MeT (e.g. E1305–6) indicate a tale which had not yet been given its final form. The second is that if Chaucer had not yet provided the tales with linking sequences, it is reasonable to suppose that he had not yet allocated the tales to a teller, for a teller is of importance only within the pilgrimage frame. Thus the inappropriateness of the teller for the tale of St Cecilia is often noted. It may have been the best the editor of Hg could do with the available pilgrims. In fact Hg identifies her only as 'The Nonne'; the 'Second' was introduced by a later editor, and is to that extent without authority. We can see again why these tales were put first because the editor had to know how much space he had for the links and he had to choose a teller for each tale from among the remaining pilgrims.

I must now justify why in my list above I grouped MLT under (ii) with the linkless tales. Its position in Hg in the section with the four other linkless tales indicates that in the copytext it was without link or named teller. MLP fits awkwardly with MLT and it has often been surmised that Chaucer wrote MLP for a different pilgrim and position in the poem. MLP is in couplets, but MLT in stanzas. The tale to follow MLP is said to be in prose (B¹ 96), but MLT is in verse. Furthermore it seems inappropriate that the man of law should give the recital of Chaucer's works found in MLP. The man of law is named once in MLP when the host addresses him as 'Sire man of lawe' at B¹ 33. If we assume for the moment that this name was inserted editorially and if we accept, as is generally done, that the running heads are also editorial, for in *IV they were added by a later hand, there is no evidence that Chaucer ever referred to this pilgrim as the 'man of law'. In Pro 309 Chaucer introduces a 'sergeaunt of lawe'. One might naturally expect this nomenclature to have been preserved by Chaucer later in the poem, as is true with the other pilgrims. The appellation 'man of law' would appear to be editorial. It may be significant that after MLP the tale is introduced simply as 'Here bigynneth the tale' with no reference to the man of law. MLP itself has the unusual heading 'The prohemie of the mannes tale of lawe', for elsewhere 'prologue' is used. This heading suggests editorial intervention.

Why then did the editor put MLP here? It does not refer back to any other tale and so fits most appropriately at the head of a section such as *IV. Since CkT was unfinished, MLP provided a good way of starting the next part of the poem. Furthermore, it contains the list of Chaucer's works and so perhaps was felt to deserve a prominent place such as the beginning of *IV. Why he gave it to the man of law must remain uncertain, though the choice among the remaining pilgrims was limited. He at least was important, knowledgeable and familiar with London. Since all the linkless tales were in verse the inconsistency of B¹ 96 was inevitable. While it is not possible to prove definitively that MLP and MLT were independent in the copytext, because they are linked in Hg and all subsequent manuscripts, I think a reasonable case can be made for that hypothesis.

In the first part of *IV the SqT–MeT and MeT–FkT gaps are

filled, but not the MLT–SqT and FkT–SNT gaps. An explanation
for this omission may depend on the relation of the editor of Hg
to other manuscripts of the poem. The early manuscripts were
produced in London or Westminster and if there was only one
copytext, as I believe, there would be cooperation among the
editors/scribes. As far as the MLT–SqT gap is concerned, it may
not be fortuitous that a piece exists which could fit there (B^1 1163–
90). This is not found in early manuscripts, but it occurs in many
later ones. Many of these read 'squire' at B^1 1179, some read
'summoner' and one reads 'shipman'. It is conceivable that the
editor of Hg had this piece composed (for the reading 'squire'
suggests it was meant as the MLT–SqT link), but decided not to
include it because a new arrangement was being considered which
made it redundant. For when D was put after MLPT (as it was in
El and manuscripts of the *a* group), there was no need for an endlink for MLT since WBP provided the necessary pilgrimage link
between these two sections. And this arrangement is foreshadowed in Hg since D was moved from its intended position
and inserted before MLPT. The scribe of Hg could not put it after
MLPT without breaking up his existing quires and this he was not
prepared to do. However, if the spurious endlink to MLT was left
with the copytext it could have been picked up by scribes writing
so much later that they did not realize it was spurious. The existence of this link may have encouraged the editor of the archetype
of group *c* to take SqT out of its position in El and put it after MLT
to which it was joined by the link. This leaves the wife of Bath
group untouched and in some ways is an improvement on El.
The authority of El might then have led some scribes to find a
replacement for 'squire' at B^1 1179. The FkT–SNT gap also
disappeared when SNT was moved to a different position; and
SNT was moved to this new position in El and manuscripts of the
a group. This move is foreshadowed by the late copying of
SNT.[1] It is surely significant that the gaps which were not filled in

---

[1] As Doyle and Parkes point out in *Facsimile* the double quire with FkT was
made because there was some uncertainty about the inclusion of SNT. They
argue that SNT was included later because of the ink colour and the system of
underlining. But if it was copied later, it is clear the scribe knew exactly how
long it was since he left the right number of folios to accommodate it. The later

Hg disappeared in later manuscripts, at least one of which had some connection with Hg; the scribe of El and Hg was the same man.

While the spurious links were being composed and *IV–III was being copied the editor of Hg changed his mind about the order and decided finally to move D forward. The reason is not far to seek. The wife of Bath is mentioned in earlier tales and so it is illogical to have WBPT near the end of the poem. That this fact was not discovered earlier is hardly surprising because the references to her are not obvious: they are found within MeT and ClT. If we remember that Hg is the earliest copy and that the editor may not have read all the fragments in their entirety before they were sent to the scribe because he was in a hurry to have it published and it is a long poem, this situation is hardly surprising. He therefore decided to put D before MLPT because that was the only place it could be fitted in before MeT and ClT without considerable rewriting. This move foreshadows what was to happen in El to which I now turn.

With two manuscripts like Hg and El it is theoretically possible that both are independent witnesses, that both descend from a common original, or that one depends on the other. Without doubt the order of the tales in all manuscripts is linked. The simi-

---

insertion of SNT cannot be used to prove that the editor did not have all the copy at the beginning. The answer to the doubt over SNT may be this. I believe that CYT is spurious because it is not in Hg; but it was clearly written early in the fifteenth century as it is found in early manuscripts like Ha⁴ and El. It is likely that the editor of Hg knew it was being written and that it was to be linked to SNT. Indeed because CYT was started before SNT was allocated to a teller, the author of CYT had to refer in his first line to the Life of St Cecilia and not to the nun. The editor kept SNT back in the hope that CYT would be ready in time. As it did not become available to meet his deadline, he told the scribe to fill in the space he had left for it. That the writing of SNT shares certain characteristics with PsT headings, which were almost certainly added at the end, indicates that the editor was prepared to wait till the very end before abandoning hope of getting the complete CYT. That CYT was written late and in haste and differs from the other tales is mentioned already in W. W. Skeat, *The Complete Works of Geoffrey Chaucer*, vol. 3 (Oxford, 1894), pp. 492–3. We may also remark that the care taken in leaving this gap proves that the editor of Hg had a system and that he did not wish to put the tales in any order.

larities among them are such that they must have a common basis. Without that shared basis there is no reason why those tales which have no localizing features, such as those in C, constantly recur in the same position in the poem. If each scribe was starting from scratch one would expect a greater diversity in the ordering of the groups. Hg and El cannot be independent witnesses. It is unlikely that Hg and El depend on a common ancestor for tale order, for the arrangement I have outlined for Hg presupposes that it was made from fragments and not from an ordered text. This in its turn indicates that Hg is the earliest published form of the poem with the corollary that El is dependent upon it or an intermediary. In fact I use El here not because it was necessarily the next published version of the poem, but because its order is taken to be the norm by modern scholars. To that extent it here represents how Hg's order was modified by later editors.

The text of El is copied out elegantly and continuously; the scribe did not make up his order as he went along. The situation facing the editor of El was different since there was already an order for the poem in existence—an order he may have had a hand in fixing. He did not need to put the various fragments together; his concern was to improve the order already available. In doing so he was motivated by two factors: the rôle of the wife of Bath and the inclusion of CYT. As the wife of Bath is the only pilgrim to be mentioned outside her own tale, it is natural that an editor should consider her important enough to affect the order. For in El WBPT and the two tales which refer to her, MeT and ClT, are brought as close together as possible. Hg's order of D and MLPT was reversed. There was no need to break up D, since the friar and the summoner participate in the wife of Bath episode. As ClT and MeT were originally independent fragments, the editor of El would have little hesitation in revising their order in Hg. The overall effect is to disrupt the existing order of Hg as little as possible. This is what one might expect, for when you have an order in front of you there is a tendency to juggle with that order rather than to arrange all the pieces again *de novo*.

The new order to emerge was MLPT, D, ClT, MeT, SqT,

FkT. As ClT has an exchange between the host and the clerk to introduce it, there was a pilgrimage link between D and ClT. But ClT had in Hg the host stanza, which may now have seemed inappropriate since it did not provide any thematic link between those tales which the new order had deliberately united. As it happens this link was kept in El, but it was omitted in other early manuscripts and a new link written; this new link was also introduced into El—probably a sign of conflation. The new link emphasized the connection between ClT and MeT. It refers to Griselda and to the merchant's shrewish wife (of which Pro says nothing). What more natural than that in writing this link the editor should take his cue from the last line of ClT. The echo between E1212 and E1213 is more satisfactorily accounted for in this way.

As MeT now followed ClT, the editor was left with SqT and FkT. He kept them in that order because that was the order in Hg, though if he had been concerned with marriage rather than the wife of Bath he might have reversed their order. The new scheme demanded a relatively simple revision of links. Hg's MeT–FkT link was changed into the MeT–SqT link with appropriate change of name and the alteration of F2; and its SqT–MeT link was changed into the SqT–FkT link again with the necessary change of name. Since these links were originally tied only closely to the tale they followed (and they still followed the same tales), the changes were straightforward. And as the editor of El knew they were spurious he had no compunction in altering them. Finally one may note that El contains extra lines in WBP (D575–84, 609–12, 619–26, 717–20) not found in Hg or other early manuscripts like Ha⁴. This may indicate three stages in the development of this new order: (1) Hg, in which the rôle of the wife of Bath is first noticed; (2) Ha⁴, in which the new order is introduced; and (3) El, in which the new order encouraged the editor to add extra lines about the wife of Bath to make her even more important in the poem.

The inclusion of CYT was relatively straightforward. It refers in its opening line to the life of St Cecilia, i.e. SNT, and so must follow that tale. In its third line it also refers to Boughton-under-

Blee, which naturally links it to the Blean forest mentioned in McP. CYT consequently attracted SNT from its original position, where it had become isolated, and both were located before McPT. CYT has no endlink, but that was of no consequence since McP, an episode from the pilgrimage frame, acted as link. But SNT now followed NPT. As in Hg SNT has no prologue and NPT no endlink, there was a hiatus between the two tales. This was not filled in El, but it was in manuscripts of the *a* group by the sixteen lines now known as NPT endlink. There is no doubt that this is a spurious link. Scribes who were unimpressed by the geographical link between CYT and McP put the new group G in the position which SNT had in Hg. They therefore had no need for the NPT endlink.

We may conclude that Hg was the first published text of the poem and that El is based on it. There was only one copytext of the poem when Chaucer died and that was more fragmentary than we previously imagined. It consisted of the thirteen sections listed under categories (i), (ii) and (iii) above. No other parts can be regarded as Chaucerian. Hg embodies a first attempt to arrange a set of apparently unrelated fragments into some coherent order. The other manuscripts embody variations on the order in Hg or subsequent manuscripts; no later editor took the fragments and started the process of arrangement from the beginning again. But from the start the editors were active in supplementing what they found; in this activity there was evidently considerable cooperation. In their arrangements the editors had not the least interest in those features of geography and chronology which have so exercised modern critics. Such aspects of realism are a modern concern. They were intent on providing a sequence of tale–link–tale, though a subsidiary interest developed while the first copy was in progress: the rôle of the wife of Bath. It does not follow that Chaucer was as interested in the wife of Bath and her rôle in the poem as the editors were or that he would have grouped the tales in the way El does—though he may have done. But that new links had to be created by the editors indicates a movement to order the poem in a way that Chaucer had not imagined. Overall the evidence shows that Chaucer had not got very far in planning the order of the tales; perhaps he had as yet no definite plan.

In this article I have referred to the editors of Hg and El and to spurious additions and it might be asked whether the editors were Chaucer and the spurious pieces simply revisions. This is a possible solution, though palaeographers date Hg after 1400 and the remark in Hg after CkT that 'Of this Cokes tale maked Chaucer namoore' implies that Chaucer was already dead. On present evidence it seems more probable that the arrangements in Hg and El are scribal.

II

Langland and the Contexts of 'Piers Plowman'

ELIZABETH SALTER

THE presentation of *Piers Plowman* in an English alliterative context throws more light upon our need for a new historical geography of the alliterative revival than it does upon our understanding of the special qualities of Langland's thought and art. The difficulty of defining the part it played in the narrative of the revival has always been apparent—although editors and critics frequently minimize, by a variety of explanations and procedures, that difficulty. We can still propose that the emergence of the A–text of *Piers Plowman* was a strong determining factor in the establishment of the alliterative line as one dominant verse-form for the rest of the fourteenth century without feeling the need to propose any close affinities, artistic or conceptual, between Langland's poem and any other major alliterative work. Comparisons, unless forced, usually serve to isolate *Piers Plowman* and nothing substantial suggests that the authors of alliterative dream-debates such as *Winner and Waster, Mum and the Sothsegger* and *Death and Life* were capable of benefiting from, even if they recognized, Langland's comprehensive and powerful grasp of issues, his deep spirituality. The metrical form of *Piers Plowman* misleads us, therefore, if it encourages us to expect to find, in the main branches of alliterative poetry, more than fleeting likenesses to Langland's sense of his function and status, and to his concept of the suiting of subject-matter to art. Indeed, we do somewhat better when we seek instead in non–alliterative verse. Chaucer's complex self-consciousness as thinker and artist put him in a different European world, but Gower's *Vox Clamantis* and *Miroir de l'Homme* share areas of content with *Piers Plowman*, even if their centres of concern are often quite different.

It is hardly controversial to say that the poem is most obviously at home among that vast collection of medieval writings, in verse and prose, which, over the thirteenth and fourteenth centuries, interpreted established doctrine—political, scientific and devotional for the benefit of the lesser clergy and the educated laity. But unspectacular though the statement may be, it provides the only sound basis for further observation. For within this wide grouping, *Piers Plowman* is not only the most eclectic product of the English Middle Ages but intelligibly so. There are, for instance, various kinds of precedent for some aspects of its strategy— its ambitious coverage of extremely diverse subject-matter, drawing upon authorities in Latin and more than one vernacular language, and its attempt to order this subject-matter into a sequence of 'passus' or books, with some attention to indicating sources and quotation for the reader. Such precedents are not predominantly found, however, in the English vernacular.

A recent article, of seminal importance to medieval studies, has drawn our attention to the *compilatio* genre of literature which, from its base in Latin works such as the *Speculum Maius* of Vincent of Beauvais, apparently exerted a much stronger influence upon vernacular writings than has hitherto been recognized.[1] Langland knew the *Speculum*—or at least that section of it entitled the *Speculum Naturale*. He probably also knew a variety of other *compilationes*, from the thirteenth century *Lumere as Lais* of Peter of Peckham to the *De Proprietatibus Rerum* of Bartholomaeus Anglicus, translated into English by John Trevisa during his own life-time. There are specific indications in the manuscripts of *Piers Plowman*—not only the careful disposition into 'passus' but also the underlining or 'boxing-in' of proper names, the underlining of quotations[2]—that Langland's scribes recognized some kind of *compilatio* format in the poem, even if it was not as elaborate or systematic an example as it could have been.

Current suggestions as to Langland's models for the overall form of *Piers Plowman*, still working with the more familiar

[1] See M. B. Parkes, 'The Influence of the Concepts of *Ordinatio* and *Compilatio* on the Development of the Book', *Medieval Learning and Literature: Essays Presented to R. W. Hunt*, ed. J. G. Alexander and M. T. Gibson (Oxford, 1976), pp. 115–41.

[2] Parkes, pp. 133–4.

literary genres of the vernacular languages, tend to concentrate on one or more of the many different strands of the poem—political and social satire, school psychology, penitential theology, apocalyptic prophecy, Christo-centric devotion—and attempt to see some kind of loose unity imposed by the frame-work of the dream. It is easy to demonstrate that, while such accounts may be accurate for certain stretches of *Piers Plowman*, there are many other stretches where Langland seems to be doing no more—and no less—than the *compilatores*: the manipulation and rearrangement of large quantities of traditional material, with an eye to their greater accessibility to varied classes of readers.

It is, in fact, useful to look further into one of the medieval texts cited by Dr. Parkes to see how the business of 'the making of books', 'modus faciendi librum', is divided into a four-fold scheme of scribe, compiler, commentator and author: as *compilator*, the writer was only responsible for the re-ordering of authoritative material and its augmentation from the work of others: the *commentator* elucidated from his own writings, but in a subordinate way: the *auctor* reversed the proportions of original and derived matter.[1] None of these terms in isolation would cover Langland all of the time, but when we try to define the differences between his concept of himself as writer and that of Chaucer, for instance, or that of the 'classical' alliterative poet, Bonaventura's description of the categories of book-making, with their interlinked activities, seems to comment helpfully upon features of Langland's attitude to his 'authorial status' which have long been thought unusual in a man who was the contemporary of Chaucer and the *Gawain* poet: his strong sense of himself as primarily a simple learner and purveyor of information, his sternly limited interest in his medium as art, his ultimate undervaluing of anything except the search for the heart of the matter. The dreamer's rather surprising identification of 'makynges' with 'bokes ... to telle men what dowel is, dobet and dobest bothe ...' and even, perhaps, with 'werk' itself,[2] becomes more easily acceptable if we understand

[1] Bonaventura, *In Primum Librum Sententiarum*, proem, quaest. iv, quoted Parkes, pp. 127–8.
[2] Passus xii, B-text, ll.16 foll.

Langland to be as often *compilator* and *commentator* as *auctor*. His much-remarked modesty is only as unusual as that of the encyclopaedist or treatise-writer; we could add 'sermonist' as long as we admit that he shuns the pedagogical assurance which characterizes some medieval preachers, imitating it merely as a special satirical device.

It will be thought that by citing encyclopaedists and treatise-writers to illustrate certain points about Langland's 'practical aesthetics', we associate him with traditions of prose rather than those of poetry. Certainly we should record both his adoption of the traditional stances of instructional literature and his adoption of a verse-form for his work—without, however, exaggerating the unusual nature of such a combination. Not only in the vernacular languages but also in Latin the interchangeability of verse and prose on all but the most learned levels of instruction is a common enough phenomenon throughout the medieval period. For an Englishman who was very likely familiar with the enormous quantity of literary composition, verse and prose, produced in Anglo-French and English as a prolonged response to the Lateran Council of 1215, the choice of one form or the other can hardly have been revolutionary. Indeed, the very nature of his metrical form, which some of us would like to see represented as flexibly as possible by editorial practice, gives Langland significant links not, as we have already said, with contemporary and highly 'poetic' alliterative compositions, but with a varied collection of earlier—and minor—verse, alliterative, rhymed, unrhymed: with types of avowed metrical 'hybrids', and with rhythmical prose itself. The roots of *Piers Plowman* spread wide and deep, drawing upon sources both humble and distinguished, without regard to their special literary character.

We have, for instance, been discussing some larger-scale Latin and Anglo-French prose and verse texts as possible models for Langland in his initial stages of planning. It is characteristic of the poem, however, that numerous little work-a-day texts present themselves as models for minor episodes: roughly alliterative, rhymed treatises such as the twelfth-century English *Poema Morale* or *Conduct of Life*, still being copied in the fourteenth century.

This treatment of penitential themes is typical of the most popular and ordinary reading-matter which could have furnished Langland with bare formulae for his 'autobiographical' passages; the moment in Passus xx (B-text, ll. 182 foll.) when Will laments how 'Elde anone after me   ·   and ouer myne heed ʒede . .', rendering him deaf and impotent, is reminiscent of the same kind of moment in the *Poema*, when the anonymous author laments how

Elde is me bistolen on . . .
Nu ich wolde & i ne may   ·   for eldes ne for unhelpe . . .
Ne may ich bi-seo me bifore   ·   for smoke ne for myste . . .[1]

But it will also be observed that the alignment of *Piers Plowman* with compositions which go about the 'makyng of books' by the most straightforward principle of informed orderliness and clarity of exposition brings into sharp focus certain quite crucial features of Langland's own method of procedure. In the first place, if Langland did sometimes envisage himself in the rôle of *compilator* or *commentator* rather than in that of *auctor*, his performance often falls short of the ideal. Orderliness and clarity are no doubt his aim, but, as he himself acknowledges at least once, they are by no means always within his powers of achievement. What successes he has are of short duration. Secondly, no charge was ever laid upon the traditional compiler or commentator to personify, and show in action, those very processes of learning and instruction by which he worked. Langland personifies constantly, and some-times with a contrary brilliance which seems to indicate the presence in him of a driving but unlocalized dissatisfaction with the methods he most wishes to employ.

It is not, of course, quite out of keeping with his essentially pragmatic and low-keyed view of his status as writer that he should turn to personification; at its simplest, it is a movement towards effectiveness of communication. But simplicity of first intent does not rule out subtlety of ultimate result. There are times in *Piers Plowman* when the urge to personify does nothing

---

[1] *Poema Morale*, ed. R. Morris and W. W. Skeat, *Specimens of Early English* (Oxford, 1882) I, ll. 18–20.

more than reveal, reluctantly, the warring tensions in Langland's view of the world and the self and a scheme of salvation which he desperately needed to recommend, as authority, to others. There are other times, however, when personification represents a totally unified process, involving the exploration of whole sequences of meaning and their transmutation into binding images of revelatory power. Only in such words can Langland's 'personification' of Piers the Plowman be described—a creature first called-up, surely, from Langland's reading and meditation upon his greatest model of all—the narrative of the *New Testament*. Familiar with that narrative, which witnesses, in the language of ordinary men, to the interpenetration of ordinary lives with the energy of miracle, he knew of divine metamorphoses within the experience of the lowliest. The humble multiplication of loaves and fishes, the practical alchemy of water into wine, were signs of a spiritual potential assured to man by the concluding miracle of the Resurrection:

> whereby are given to us exceeding great and precious promises, that by these ye might be partakers of the divine nature, having escaped the corruption that is in the world through lust.
> (2 Pet. 1:4)

Though he may have strengthened his reading from more sophisticated sources, a knowledge of the *New Testament* alone could have suggested to Langland the deep mystery at the centre of appearances. His dreamer, watching Piers the Plowman assume different forms and different relationships—to Christ, to St Peter, to the Good Samaritan—and questioning what is in front of his very eyes, 'Is Piers in this place?' (Passus XVIII, B-text, l.21) is an echo of the disciples questioning Christ in wonder and perplexity: 'Some say thou art John the Baptist, some Elias, and others Jeremias or one of the prophets . . .' (Matt. 16:14) Nothing could better prepare us for the mysterious interventions of Piers than the account of Christ's appearances after the Resurrection: 'And their eyes were opened and they knew him, and he vanished out of their sight.' (Luke 24:31)

Any attempt to assign *Piers Plowman* to one dominant medieval literary tradition is doomed to failure; we have noted above how even an association with the *compilatio* form has a real but limited usefulness, serving to define Langland's departure from the norm as much as his indebtedness to it. His only *declared* allegiance is to a tradition—more conceptual than literary—of pursuing the truth, and this tradition accepts the help of whatever texts and authors may be available. This is why there is no end to the search for medieval literature and literary forms which may have shaped the three versions of his life's work: we should not reject the plainest metrical paraphrase of the Scriptures nor the rarest epistle on the spiritual life as sustenance for his journeying.[1]

[1] It is startling to find, for instance, in the Latin of Walter Hilton's *Letter to a Solitary*, an analysis of spiritual problems which could often serve as a close commentary on the problems of the dreamer, in *Piers Plowman*. The earlier date now proposed for the death of Hilton would make Langland's knowledge of his writings even more likely. See the translation of *A Letter* by Joy Russell-Smith, in *The Way*, vol. 6 (1966).

III

Eating and Drinking in 'Piers Plowman'

JILL MANN

Grex fidelis triplici cibo sustentetur,
corpore Dominico, quo fides augetur,
sermonis compendio, quod discrete detur,
mundano cibario, ne periclitetur.[1]

When we think of metaphor or of allegory (which can defensibly
be glossed as narrative metaphor),[2] we tend to assume that it
illuminates the complex by means of the simple—that it seeks to
express the elusive mysteries of the emotions and the spirit by
using the familiar features of the concrete physical world we
know and understand. It is the purpose of this essay to explore one
particular aspect of Langland's use of metaphor and allegory, the

---

[1] These lines occur in the (12th–13th c.) poem 'Viri venerabiles, sacerdotes
Dei', printed by B. Hauréau, *Notices et Extraits de Quelques Manuscrits Latins de la
Bibliothèque Nationale* vol. 6 (Paris, 1893), p. 14. They may serve as a small
indication of the extensive use of the images of eating and drinking in medieval
Latin poetry. This essay is a preliminary version of part of a book on some
aspects of allegory, language, metaphor and concept in *Piers Plowman* on which
I am at present working, and in which I hope to be able to include fuller consideration of the rich background for these metaphors in medieval Latin and
vernacular literature. Some general studies which may usefully be cited here are
Klaus Lange, 'Geistliche Speise', *Zeitschrift für Deutsches Altertum*, 95 (1966),
81–122, and the chapter on 'Banquet Imagery' in Mikhail Bakhtin, *Rabelais and
his World*, trans. H. Iswolsky (Cambridge, Mass., 1968), pp. 278–302. A. C.
Spearing has discussed the development of the theme of hunger in the C-text
from the episode of Hunger in Passus IX, with its emphasis on physical food, to
the speech of Activa-vita and Patience's reply to it in Passus XVI, which shifts
the emphasis on to the spiritual aspect of the problem of food ('The Development of a Theme in *Piers Plowman*', *Review of English Studies*, n.s. 11, 1960,
241–53). Elizabeth Kirk has also pointed to the importance of the images of food
and drink, both physical and spiritual, in the poem (*The Dream Thought of
Piers Plowman* New Haven and London, 1972, pp. 132–3, 153 and 197).

[2] See the beginning of the stimulating chapter on allegory in Pamela Gradon,
Form and Style in Early English Literature (London, 1971), pp. 32–92.

images of eating and drinking in *Piers Plowman*, in order to show that in his poetry the material world is not merely a vehicle for expressing the immaterial, but on the contrary contains the heart of its meaning and its mystery. If on the one hand the material world is interpenetrated by a spiritual reality which transcends material laws, on the other hand the laws of the material world interpenetrate spiritual reality and resolve some of its most fundamental problems.

As a consequence, this discussion must include Langland's representation of actual hunger and thirst, and actual eating and drinking, as well as their more obviously metaphorical applications, and I use the term 'image' as one which will cover both metaphorical and concrete uses. It is, of course, largely due to the general structure of the allegory that we can see even the most apparently concrete activities as metaphorical, and vice versa. In the lengthy account of the ploughing of Piers' half-acre in Passus VI, it might seem that Langland is primarily concerned with the concrete rôles of the real members of fourteenth-century society in the production and consumption of food—but because the ploughing which was meant to be a prelude to the pilgrimage to Treuthe eventually comes to be seen as an allegorical replacement for it, it acts as nourishment for the spirit as well as the body. Conversely, when in Passus XIX (260 ff.) we hear of Piers 'ploughing' with the four evangelists as his oxen, and sowing in man's heart the seeds of the four cardinal virtues, it might seem that only spiritual food is in question; but the harvest of this sowing is celebrated in the Eucharist, which offers bodily as well as spiritual refreshment:

'Cometh', quod Conscience · ' ȝe Cristene, and dyneth,
That han laboured lelly ·   al this lente-tyme.
Here is bred yblessed ·   and goddes body ther-vnder.'[1]

(381–3)

---

[1] All quotations are from the B-text unless it is otherwise stated. I cite from W. W. Skeat's two-volume edition (Oxford, 1886), with occasional corrections from the edition of the B-text by G. Kane and E. T. Donaldson (London, 1975).

Often, however, Langland is not content to rely on the structure
of the allegory, and adopts special means to make us simultane-
ously conscious of both real and metaphorical dimensions for the
image, as in his complaint of the avarice of 'chapeleynes':

> Vnkynde to her kyn · and to alle cristene,
> Chewen here charite · and chiden after more.
>
> (I. 190–1)

Metaphorically, the chaplains are greedy of their charity—wish,
'cormorant-like', to swallow it up for themselves—but the image
also suggests that they do so by actually eating food which they
could give to others. It is easy to see from these instances the difficulties in dividing Langland's food and drink images into concrete
or metaphorical, bodily *or* spiritual. But for the sake of conveni-
ence in discussion, I shall start with those images which seem to
have most emphasis on the concrete; secondly, move on to
more metaphorical usages; and finally, show how even the most
apparently metaphorical examples ultimately resolve themselves
into concretions.

One of the most important aspects of the concrete production
of food is its socializing rôle, which Mikhail Bakhtin has sum-
marized as follows:

> In the oldest system of images food was related to work. It
> concluded work and struggle and was their crown of glory.
> Work triumphed in food. Human labour's encounter with the
> world and the struggle against it ended in food, in the swallow-
> ing of that which had been wrested from the world. As the last
> victorious stage of work, the image of food often symbolized
> the entire labour process . . . It must be stressed that both labour
> and food were collective; the whole of society took part in
> them. Collective food as the conclusion of labour's collective
> process was not a biological, animal act but a social event.
>
> (*Rabelais and his World*, p. 281)

So we may begin discussion of the importance of concrete food in
Piers Plowman by looking at its rôle in the formation and regula-

tion of social relationships in the ploughing of Piers' half-acre in
Passus VI. In the course of the ploughing, the various social groups
define themselves and their relationships to each other (see especially ll. 7–97). Moreover, although in providing food for those
'that feithfulliche libbeth' (71), Piers and his fellows serve Treuthe,
it is not only obedience to Treuthe which acts as stimulus to their
labour; it is the simple driving force of natural needs. We see this
clearly when some of the lazier workers refuse to continue, and the
knight's attempts to coerce them prove fruitless; only Piers'
summons of Hunger is effective.

Hunger in haste tho　·　hent Wastour bi the mawe,
And wronge hym so bi the wombe　·　that bothe his eyen
                                                  wattered;
He buffeted the Britoner　·　aboute the chekes,
That he loked like a lanterne　·　al his lyf after.
                                              (176–9)

The control of this society is not solely in the hands of its human
members. They depend on the power of Hunger to drive them
to work—and in that sense Hunger plays a beneficial rôle in
society. But Hunger is not always so conveniently subservient to
human interests; once installed in society he refuses to depart,
and eventually has to be put to sleep with a whole banquet of
homely fare, which Langland clearly enjoys enumerating with
concrete specificity: 'two grene cheses', 'A fewe cruddes and
creem　·　and an hauer cake', 'percil and porettes　·　and many
kole-plantes', 'Benes and baken apples', 'Chibolles and cheruelles
·　and ripe chiries manye' (283–97). The society envisaged in this
Passus is thus not ruled solely by moral laws—nor even by the
physical coercion exerted by one social group on another. It is
ruled, ultimately, by the laws of physical nature. Natural laws
may embrace moral laws, but they cannot be confined to them;
Hunger cannot be summoned and dismissed as morally appropriate even though his rôle may have a morally appropriate effect
(the punishment of wasters).

One conclusion that can be drawn from this episode is that
Langland sees justice as naturally 'built in to' the world. He does

not quote the biblical text 'If any would not work, neither should he eat' (2 Thess. 3:10), but it is clearly fundamental to his thought. But if justice is thus an inherent part of the nature of things, rather than humanly or divinely imposed, how can it ever fall into abeyance?—as it clearly does when Hunger is finally put to sleep and the wasters take over. Partly, this state of affairs is due to the fact that individual human beings can pervert nature by the sin of gluttony, which overrides the moderation that nature would dictate. (The cloak of Hawkin the Active Man is soiled with Gluttony because he has eaten and drunk more 'then kende miȝt defie'.[1]) But partly it is due to the possibility for wasters to live off the labour of others, to win food by begging. So Langland introduces a long discussion between Hunger and Piers on the question of whether Piers is perverting justice and nature if he gives food to those who do not work. The problem is of more than local interest, since it forms part of the larger problem of how mercy can be exercised without undermining justice, which occupies Langland throughout the poem. Hunger's answer to Piers on this question is that beggars *should* be given food (albeit only coarse food), if they are needy.

'And alle maner of men ·   that thow myȝte asspye,
That nedy ben, and nauȝty ·   helpe hem with thi godis,
Loue hem and lakke hem nouȝte ·   late god take the veniaunce.'[2]
(225–7)

It is need which thus creates the suspension of vengeance. Need overrides the dispensation of reward and punishment according to moral deserts; physical need takes precedence over moral laws. And it is hunger that teaches us this.

The lines quoted above, however, are hardly sufficient by themselves to indicate the importance of need, and Langland gives it independent treatment in a very curious and isolated incident at the beginning of Passus xx. The dreamer is looking for some-

[1] xIII. 404. In the C-text, this line forms part of Gluttony's confession (vII. 430).

[2] Kane and Donaldson's text differs considerably at this point, but the references to need and vengeance are unaffected.

where to eat, and being unable to find anywhere, around midday
he appropriately meets Need. Need berates him for failing to
provide for his physical requirements by any means available, as
would be legitimate if he took no more than Need taught him, for

'.. Nede ne hath no lawe · ne neure shal falle in dette
For thre thynges he taketh · his lyf forto saue,
That is, mete, whan men hym werneth · and he no money
                                                    weldeth,
Ne wyght none wil ben his borwe · ne wedde hath none to
                                                    legge.
And he cauʒte in that cas · and come ther-to by sleighte,
He synneth nouʒte sothelich · that so wynneth his fode.
And though he come so to a clothe · and can no better
                                                    cheuysaunce,
Nede anon riʒte · nymeth hym vnder meynpryse.
And if hym lyst for to lape · the lawe of kynde wolde
That he dronke at eche diche · ar he for thurste deyde.
So Nede at grete nede · may nymen as for his owne,
Wyth-oute conseille of Conscience · or cardynale vertues,
So that he suwe and saue · *spiritus temperancie*.'[1]

                                                    (10–22)

Need continues to define himself for another twenty-five lines,
and the dreamer then falls asleep—leaving this little episode without an obvious sequel, as it is without an obvious introduction. Its
full significance will only become clear later; for the moment it
may stand as demonstration that Langland's reference to need in
Passus IV is not a casual one, but part of a clearly-thought out conception of the relationship between physical and moral laws.

In the C-text, Langland's insistence that no one should beg
'bote yf he haue nede' leads to a description of the life of the needy
which is an excellent example of his fully concrete realization of

---

[1] The punctuation of line 10 follows Kane and Donaldson's edition; Skeat's
punctuation is clearly wrong. The images of debt, pledge and bail ('meynpryse')
strengthen the link (which I shall be suggesting later) between this passage and
the account of the Harrowing of Hell in Pasus XVIII (see esp. ll. 182–5). An
excellent and illuminating study of the legal imagery in *Piers Plowman* is to be
found in Dr. Anna Baldwin's unpublished Ph.D. dissertation (Cambridge 1975),
'The Law of the King in the C-text of Piers Plowman', to which I am much
indebted; on debt, surety and 'mainprise', see esp. pp. 118–42.

hunger and thirst (Cx. 71–97). Langland does not try to win our sympathy for the poor by directly describing them and their pitiful appearance (as does, for example, his less sensitive follower, the author of *Pierce the Ploughmans Crede*, in his picture of the poor ploughman);[1] instead, he makes poetry out of the things that make up the lives of the poor, and thus re-creates the texture of those lives around us as we read. Their bareness, their pinched quality can be felt especially in the concrete details of food and drink: 'papelotes' made of 'mylk' and 'mele', 'To a-glotye with here gurles · that greden after fode', 'payn and peny-ale', 'Colde flessh and colde fyssh', 'a ferthyng-worth of muscles .. other so fele cockes' (Cx. 75–6, 92–5). The poverty of the poor is most clearly shown in the simple fact that they are *not there* in the lines describing their lives; they are, as it were, only the emptiness which is filled up with the daily round of wearing tasks and pitiful items of food and drink. The spare, matter-of-fact tone registers the fact that even emotion is a luxury which the poor cannot afford, so that we are left to confront hunger in its most concrete and simple reality:

> Al-so hem-selue · suffren muche hunger ...
> Both a-fyngrede and a-furst · to turne the fayre outwarde,
> And beth abashed for to begge · and wolle nat be aknowe
> What hem needeth at here neihebores · at non and at euen.
> (Cx. 77, 85–7)

Such passages work cumulatively to establish hunger and thirst, food and drink as subjects of major importance in the poem. It is only when we see them as subjects in their own right that we can properly understand, for example, Langland's frequent outbursts against those social classes that are guilty of corrupting food—'Brewesteres and bakesteres · bocheres and cokes' who

> ... rychen thorw regraterye · and rentes hem buggen
> With that the pore people · shulde put in here wombe.
> (III. 78, 83–4)

---

[1] Ed. W. W. Skeat, EETS, o.s. 30 (London, 1867), ll. 422–7.

—and who would otherwise seem rather minor villains to be singled out for attack. We also might interpret as merely 'conventional' the recurrent denunciations of gluttony, such as the following one which emerges, to our surprise, in the middle of an elaborate explanation of Inwitte:

> Moche wo worth that man · that mys-reuleth his Inwitte,
> And that be glotouns globbares · her god is her wombe;
> > *Quorum deus venter est.*
> For thei seruen Sathan · her soule shal he haue;
> That liueth synful lyf here · her soule is liche the deuel.
> And alle that lyuen good lyf · aren like god almiȝti;
> > *Qui manet in caritate, in deo manet, &c.*
>
> (IX. 59–63)

The importance of food in this passage becomes even clearer if we take into account Skeat's comment (vol. 2, p. 141) that the text 'Qui manet in caritate . . .' (1 John 4:16) 'was commonly repeated in the Graces before and after meat'.[1] The importance of food and drink in the poem similarly explains why Gluttony is given the most vivid and elaborate of the confessions of the Seven Deadly Sins; Langland wishes to develop an image of the dissipating and futile nature of gluttony which will serve as a powerful contrast to the rôle of hunger in regulating productive work and social interchange.[2] Further, food and drink enter into the portraits of all the other sins except the half-dozen lines devoted to Pride. Lecher's short confession includes a vow of fasting. Envy suffers from indigestion—

> I myȝte nouȝte eet many ȝeres · as a man ouȝte,
> For enuye and yuel wille · is yuel to defye.
>
> (V. 120–1)

Wrath works in a convent kitchen as 'potagere' and 'cooks up' quarrels out of gossip and slander: 'Of wikked wordes I, Wrath ·

---

[1] Skeat also notes (vol. 2, p. 207) several other Latin texts used as graces which are quoted by Langland.

[2] Cf. the picture of gluttony frustrating social order and productivity at Prol. 22.

here wortes i-made' (v. 157–64); conversely, he is 'starved out' of monasteries by 'vnthende fisshe · and fieble ale drynke' (177). Avarice and his wife are corrupters of ale (v. 219–25), and Sloth concludes his confession by acknowledging that he has let food go to waste through his laziness (v. 442–5).

Wrath's rôle as cook, making 'wortes' out of 'wordes', serves to introduce us to a major metaphorical use of the image of eating and drinking—the idea of eating words. The associative connection between food and speech is something almost entirely lost to us, except in such unthinkingly-used phrases as 'I'll make him eat his words' or 'he swallowed the story whole'. But in the Middle Ages the two functions of the mouth were much more commonly related to each other, and a traditional cluster of ideas and imagery expressed this connection.[1] In medieval English literature, we have only to think of Chaucer's *Pardoner's Tale* (which the Pardoner cannot tell until he has had a drink), and its use of the mouth (the Pardoner's flow of rhetoric) to castigate the sins of the mouth (gluttony and oaths) to see the strength and integration of the tradition.[2] The connection does not just reside in the notion that the mouth takes in food and 'spews up' words; it has, for example, a simple experiential foundation in the fact that the table is a place for talk, and drink loosens a man's tongue. Speech accompanies eating and drinking and is influenced by them. The consequence of this is that a perversion in eating and drinking leads to a perversion in words, and vice versa. In a long passage at the beginning of Passus X we can see many aspects of this idea. Dame Study attacks contemporary lords for preferring to be entertained at dinner by the base kind of minstrels that

> Spitten and spewen · and speke foule wordes,
> Drynken and dryuelen · and do men for to gape.
> (40–1)

[1] See Bakhtin, *Rabelais and his World*, pp. 283–6.
[2] See John Leyerle, 'Thematic Interlace in "The Canterbury Tales"', *Essays and Studies*, 29 (1976), pp. 113–14, on the importance of food and drink in the *Pardoner's Tale*, and cf. F. Tupper, 'Chaucer's Sinners and Sins', *Journal of English and Germanic Philology*, 15 (1916), pp. 67–71, on the tale's use of the traditional medieval links between gluttony, swearing and blasphemy.

—instead of one that 'hath holy writte · ay in his mouth' (32). In addition, the clerks who share in these feasts practise a kind of verbal *gourmandise*:

> Thanne telleth thei of the trinite · a tale other tweyne,
> And bringen forth a balled resoun · and taken Bernard to
> witnesse,
> And putten forth a presumpsioun · to preue the sothe.
> Thus thei dryuele at her deyse · the deite to knowe,
> And gnawen god with the gorge · whan her gutte is fulle.
>
> (x. 53–7)

And the new and perverted habit of eating meals in private rooms (and thus denying the social importance of food, the benefit to the community from meals in hall which can be shared by travellers or beggars) leads lords themselves, 'etyng atte table', to 'Carpen as thei clerkes were · of Cryste and of his miȝtes', and to quibble over theological doctrines in 'crabbed wordes' (x. 96 ff.).

There is however yet another connection—and a more purely metaphorical one—which is described in Jean Leclercq's book on the culture of medieval monasticism, *The Love of Learning and the Desire for God*.[1] He is commenting on the significance of the medieval habit of reading texts aloud, rather than silently to oneself:

> This repeated mastication of the divine words is sometimes described by use of the theme of spiritual nutrition. In this case the vocabulary is borrowed from eating, from digestion, and from the particular form of digestion belonging to the ruminants. For this reason, reading and meditation are sometimes described by the very expressive word *ruminatio* ... To meditate is to attach oneself closely to the sentence being recited and weigh all its words in order to sound the depths of their full meaning. It means assimilating the content of a text by means of a kind of mastication which releases its full flavour. It means, as St Augustine, St Gregory, John of Fécamp and others say in an untranslatable expression, to taste it with the *palatum cordis* or *in ore cordis*. (pp. 89–90)

[1] Translated by C. Misrahi (New York, 1974) originally printed as *L'Amour des Lettres et le Désir de Dieu* (Paris, 1957).

It is not necessary to assume that Langland was or had ever been a monk (although aspects of his work which suggest monastic connections have been commented on in the past)[1] to envisage his being familiar with the notion thus described, and his having memorized and contemplated many passages of scripture in this way. His poem itself makes clear that Langland had meditated on a large number of biblical texts—and also on their relationship to each other, so that one text called another to mind in a manner that habitual contemplation and study of the Bible made natural.[2] Leclercq claims that the monks were so deeply imbued with the text of scripture that they had no need of artificial aids to underpin the development of their associative stream of thought. But such aids did, nevertheless, exist, in the form of the so-called *distinctiones*. These aids to biblical study 'amount to alphabetical concordances of key words from Scripture ... accompanied by citations or quotations from the Biblical text', which 'served as a guide to the Biblical *sentence* of important objects or conceptions'.[3]

[1] See Morton W. Bloomfield's article 'Was William Langland a Benedictine Monk?', *Modern Language Quarterly*, 4 (1943), 57–61. Bloomfield's book, *Piers Plowman as a Fourteenth-Century Apocalypse* (New Brunswick, New Jersey, 1961) is a more general discussion of the influence of monastic ways of thinking (*Denkform*) on Langland's poem. (This book is hereafter cited as *Apocalypse*.)

[2] Cf. John A. Alford's article on the influence of such meditation on Richard Rolle's prose style: 'Biblical *Imitatio* in the Writings of Richard Rolle', ELH, 40 (1973), 1–23. Alford's unpublished dissertation, '*Piers Plowman* and the Tradition of biblical *Imitatio*' (Univ. of North Carolina, 1969) was unfortunately not available to me.

[3] D. W. Robertson Jr and Bernard F. Huppé, *Piers Plowman and Scriptural Tradition* (Princeton, New Jersey, 1951), p. 5. Robertson and Huppé have related the content of the *distinctiones* (and to some extent their method) to *Piers Plowman*. See also A. C. Spearing's comment that those familiar with the *distinctiones* 'would surely have seen many common Scriptural images as exemplifying themes, and hence as pregnant with potential meanings' (*art. cit.*, *Review of English Studies* n.s. 11, 1960, p. 252).

For printed texts of *distinctiones*-collections, see: *Spicilegium Solesmense*, ed. J. B. Pitra, vols. 2–3 (Paris, 1855), in which extracts from Peter the Chanter and the *Distinctiones monasticae* are printed in conjunction with the so-called *Clavis S. Melitonis; Allegoriae in Universam Sacram Scripturam* (Ps.-Rabanus; see A. Wilmart, *Revue Bénédictine*, 32 (1920), 47–56, *PL*, 112. 849–1088; Alan of Lille, *Distinctiones Dictionum Theologicalium*, *PL*, 210. 685–1012. See also C. Spicq, *Esquisse d'une Histoire de l'Eexégèse Latine au Moyen Age* (Paris, 1944), pp. 175–7, and Beryl Smalley, *The Study of the Bible in the Middle Ages* (2nd edn., Oxford, 1952), pp. 247–8.

Headings such as 'Fames', 'Sitis', 'Cibus', 'Esca', 'Vinum', 'Vinea', etc., appear regularly in collections of *distinctiones*. The entry under 'Cibus' in the twelfth-century *distinctiones* of Peter the Chanter will give an idea of their method:

> Cibus vel esca est voluntatis, de quo Christus dicit: 'Meus, etc.'—Animae, in Christo, scilicet contemplatio divinitatis, a quo numquam jejunavit Christus; unde: 'Providebam Dominum in conspectu meo semper.'—Scripturae; unde: 'Non in solo pane vivit homo.'—Humanae conversationis, a quo jejunavit in passione, quia nullum sibi praeter unum latronem incorporavit, de quo dicitur: 'Et operui in jejunio animam meam.'—Corporalis, a quo jejunavit Christus; unde: 'Quum jejunasset quadraginta diebus, etc.'—Incipientium, in poenitentia; unde: 'Fuerunt mihi lacyrmae panes die ac nocte.'—Proficientium, in sacra Scriptura; unde: 'Sedisti ad mensam? vide qualia apposita sunt tibi, et scito quod talia oportet te praeparare.'—Et in Eucharistia; unde: 'Probet autem se homo, etc.'—Pervenientium, in aeterna refectione; unde: 'Ut edatis et bibatis super mensam meam.'[1]

Whichever collection of *distinctiones* Langland knew—Peter's, or that of his contemporary Alan of Lille, or the thirteenth-century *Distinctiones monasticae*, or yet another—the influence of their structure is fundamental to his meditation on the many biblical texts which involve the ideas of eating and drinking, hunger and thirst. The importance of eating is therefore twofold: firstly it is metaphorically applied to the texts in the practice of *ruminatio*, and secondly, the texts which are thus 'digested' are themselves passages which use the images of eating and drinking.

We can see a vivid animation of the concept of *ruminatio* in the description of the dinner-party at Conscience's house in Passus XIII. The 'doctoure on the heigh dese' eats real food, 'mortrewes and puddynges, / Wombe-cloutes and wylde braune ·

---

[1] Ed. Pitra, vol. 3, pp. 256–7. The biblical texts cited are the following: John 4:34 (cf. *PPl*, XIV. 48 and XV. 174): Matt. 4:41; Luke 4:4 (quoted at *PPl*, XIV 46); Ps. 68:11; Matt. 4:2; Ps. 41:4 (quoted at *PPl*, VII. 123); cf. Prov. 23:1; I Cor. 11:28; Luke 22:30.

& egges yfryed with grece' (62–3). But Patience and the dreamer
are nourished by the text of scripture; they eat words.

> And than he brou3t vs forth a mees of other mete   ·   of *Mis-*
> *erere–mei–deus*;
> And he brou3te vs of *Beati-quorum*   ·   *of Beatus-virres* makynge,
> *Et-quorum-tecta-sunt-*   ·   *peccata* in a disshe
> Of derne shrifte, *Dixi*   ·   and *confitebor tibi!*
>
> (52–5)

This whole scene could itself be seen as the result of Langland's
meditation on the text: 'Man shall not live by bread alone, but by
every word that proceedeth out of the mouth of God' (Matt.
4:4; Luke 4:4). Such texts often provide a sort of 'hidden structure' in the poem, organizing and articulating its development—
or at the very least, they are nodal points which serve both to
generate and concentrate its ideas.[1] Thus, behind the description of
Charity's livelihood—

> *Fiat-voluntas-tua*   ·   fynt hym euer-more
> And if he soupeth, eet but a soppe   ·   of *spera-in-deo.*
>
> (xv. 174–5)

—is the scriptural text: 'Jesus saith unto them, "My meat is to do
the will of him that sent me"' (John 4:34). And in the famous
scene where Piers tears the pardon and renounces his concern for
his 'bely-ioye', he quotes from the Psalms (Vulgate 41:4) to mark
the transition to a new kind of food:

> *Fuerunt michi lacrime mee panes die ac nocte.*
>
> (VII. 117–23)

Yet spiritual food never supersedes real food in importance, as
we see, for example, in Langland's formulation of the duties of
bishops:

[1] Cf. Alford, *art. cit.*, 12, and Bloomfield, *Apocalypse*, pp. 30–32.

... Ysaie of ʒow speketh · and Osyas bothe,
That no man schuld be bischope · but if he hadde bothe,
Bodily fode and gostly fode · and gyue ther it nedeth;
   In domo mea non est panis neque vestimentum, et ideo nolite constit-
                                              uere me regem.
Ozias seith for such · that syke ben and fieble,
   Inferte omnes decimas in oreum meum, vt sit cibus in domo mea.
                                              (xv. 565–8)

All these aspects of the images of eating and drinking find their
richest concentration and expression in Langland's meditation on
the central mysteries of Christianity—the sin of Adam and Eve, its
redemption by the crucifixion of Christ, and the participation of
Christians in that redemption through the Eucharist. And here we
shall see how the concrete aspect of the images of eating and drinking asserts itself again. We may begin with the image of Christ's
redemption as satisfying the thirst of the sinful:

For Cryste cleped vs alle · come if we wolde,
Sarasenes and scismatikes · and so he dyd the Iewes,
   O vos omnes scicientes, venite, &c.;
And badde hem souke for synne · saufly at his breste,
And drynke bote for bale · brouke it who so myʒte.
                                              (xi. 114–17)

Christ is here presented as ministering to our spiritual thirst. And
in Passus v (in a passage which anticipates in miniature compass
the themes, images and action of the Harrowing of Hell in Passus
xviii), he is presented as ministering to our spiritual hunger.

The sonne for sorwe ther-of · les syʒte for a tyme
Aboute mydday whan most liʒte is · and mele tyme of seintes;
Feddest with thi fresche blode · owre forfadres in derknesse.
                                              (499–501)

(The passage is prefaced by the text 'Qui manet in caritate', which
acts as a kind of grace before this 'meal', and it is followed by the
text 'Verbum caro factum est'—the Word becomes flesh, and thus

people can eat it.) The power of the lines I have quoted arises not only from the matter-of-factness which aligns this with everyday (and therefore real) meal-times, but also from the double reference in the word 'fresche'; fresh in the sense of 'recently poured forth', and fresh in the sense of 'not stale'. In the painful fusion of our responses to fresh food and our responses to fresh blood, we can feel both the relief offered and the pain of its cost; but the sharpness of the sensation arises from the way the image causes us to apprehend this food as a concrete experience.

And the drinking of Christ's blood, the eating of his body, is not a metaphorical notion only; in the service of the Mass, it is actually performed. God's grace enters the body through the physical act of eating and drinking.[1] The sin of Adam and Eve was also a physical action: 'Adam and Eue · eten apples vnrosted' (v. 612)—the homely addition of 'vnrosted' makes these *real* apples to us.[2] It may be objected that this is to concentrate merely on the outward performance of their sin, which was really constituted by the desire to 'be as gods, knowing good and evil' (Gen. 2:5). It is certainly true that Langland attributes their action to this desire:

Coueytise to kunne · and to knowe science
Pulte out of paradys · Adam and Eue;
   Science appetitus hominem inmortalitatis gloria spoliauit.
And riȝte as hony is yuele to defye · and engleymeth the mawe,
Riȝt so that thorw resoun · wolde the rote knowe
Of god and of his grete myȝtes · his graces it letteth.
For in the lykyng lith a pryde · and a lycames coueitise,
Aȝein Crystes conseille · and alle clerkes techyng,
   That is, *non plus sapere quam oportet sapere.*

                      (xv. 61–7)

But it is not just that Langland uses a metaphor of eating (from Prov. 25:27)—the indigestibility of honey—to describe the consequences of an excessive desire for knowledge; it is that the image of eating is actually *contained in* the desire to know, since it

[1] Notice also that the Eucharist is, like other food, to be taken at need (xix. 387).
[2] Cf. the description of their sin as a sin of eating at xviii. 189 ff.

is an *appetite* (*'appetitus sciencie'*) and since the Latin verb *sapere* means first 'to taste' and only secondly 'to know'. The desire to know is thus a 'lycames coueitise'—a bodily desire. Thus when the dreamer expresses a desire to eat an apple from the Tree of Charity to see 'what sauoure it hadde'—to 'know' it in the Latin sense (XVI. 74)—there is, I think, nothing in his desire which is sinful or absurd. The only way you can know apples, for Langland, is to eat them.

If the desire to know is an appetite, in order to understand it we must go back to everything we have learned from the poem about concrete appetites (real hunger, real thirst). One thing we learned was that they were natural forces—driving needs which can legitimate otherwise illicit actions in finding their fulfilment. This is of crucial importance in understanding the Harrowing of Hell Passus and its justification of salvation. Righteousness insists that the sin of Adam and Eve carries eternal punishment as a natural consequence of eating the apple:

'. . . late hem chewe as thei chose · and chyde we nou3t,
sustres,
For it is botelees bale · the bite that thei eten.'
(XVIII. 199-200)

But Peace argues against this. Firstly, she says that Adam had to learn to know 'wel' by learning 'wo', just as the knowledge of hunger gives us the capacity to recognize its satisfaction (XVIII. 203-5). But secondly, and surprisingly, we find that God too had to go through this process of learning, 'to see the sorwe of dey-inge':

'And after god auntred hym-self · and toke Adames kynde,
To wyte what he hath suffred · in thre sondri places,
Both in heuene, and in erthe · and now til helle he thynketh,
To wite what al wo is · that wote of al Ioye.'
(220-3)

The union of God and man in 'kynde' means that they are united in their thirst for knowledge. The appetite for knowledge which drove man to sin drives God to redeem him, since it sends him down to earth to become flesh and die.[1]

The rôle of appetite is merely implicit in these references to the desire for knowledge. But it is made explicit when Christ himself proclaims to Lucifer the redemption of souls.

> For I, that am lorde of lyf · loue is my drynke,
> And for that drynke to-day · I deyde vpon erthe.
> I fauȝte so, me threstes ȝet · for mannes soules sake;
> May no drynke me moiste · ne my thruste slake,
> Tyl the vendage falle · in the vale of Iosepath,
> That I drynke riȝte ripe must · *resurreccio mortuorum*,
> And thanne shal I come as a kynge · crouned with angeles,
> And han out of helle · alle mennes soules.
>
> (363–70)

Behind the image of the champion of the vintage lies the beginning of Isa. 63:

> 1 Who is this that cometh from Edom, with dyed garments from Bozrah? this that is glorious in his apparel, travelling in the greatness of his strength: I that speak in righteousness, mighty to save.
> 2 Wherefore art thou red in thine apparel, and thy garments like him that treadeth in the winefat?
> 3 I have trodden the winepress alone; and of the people there was none with me: for I will tread them in mine anger, and trample them in my fury; and their blood shall be sprinkled upon my garments, and I will stain all my raiment.
> 4 For the day of vengeance is in mine heart, and the year of my redeemed is come.[2]

---

[1] See the important article of Sister Mary Clemente Davlin, '*Kynde Knowyng* as a Major Theme in *Piers Plowman* B', *Review of English Studies*, n.s. 22 (1971), 1–19, in which she argues that '*Kynde knowyng* is not only man's goal; it is God's as well' (p. 13), but does not bring out the strange similarity thus created between God's 'curiosity' and that of Adam and Eve.

[2] Langland probably also had in mind the apocalyptic vintage of Apoc. 14:15, but there too the predominant idea is of the wrath of God.

I think that the reason that Langland incorporates this passage into the Harrowing of Hell Passus, where justice and mercy are to be reconciled, is his 'rumination' on the hidden connection between its picture of God treading the 'grapes of wrath' in fury and in vengeance, and the lyrical gentleness of the immediately following passage in Isaiah: 'I will mention the lovingkindnesses of the Lord . . .'. But in Isaiah there is no mention of thirst, or of drink. Yet once this text has been 'digested', it becomes clear that it is possible to see as mysteriously present in it the simple fact that if one treads the vintage, it is because one wants drink. From the grapes of wrath flows the wine of lovingkindness. Langland discovers this as the deep and hidden impulse behind Isaiah's words, not by reflecting on them alone, but by juxtaposing them with another scriptural text, which is quoted at this point in the C-text: the gospel account of Christ's words from the cross—'Sicio', 'I thirst'. The God whom we have previously seen as offering drink to the thirsty is now himself one of the thirsting—and not metaphorically, but in the most cruel reality. And Langland suggests, I think, that the reasons for the crucifixion and redemption can only be understood as thirst. He does not offer us an abstract explanation made vivid by a concrete image; the concretion is the heart of his conception of the redemption. For if the desire to know is an appetite, so is love, as the very first Passus of the poem had made clear to us; it is an appetite which cannot be resisted until it has 'of the erthe yeten his fylle' (1. 152) and magically transformed earth into itself. God is driven by a need which is as concrete, as impossible to paraphrase, as the need of hunger or thirst. And it is, finally, this need which legitimates the suspension of the letter of the law that would leave mankind in damnation, because, as we have seen, 'need ne hath no lawe'. The daring of Langland's imagination is nowhere more clearly seen than in the way he legitimates the redemption not by man's need, but by God's.

IV

Cresseid's Trial: A Revision.
Fame and Defamation in Henryson's
'Testament of Cresseid'

GÖTZ SCHMITZ

THE one feature of Henryson's *Testament of Cresseid* that stuck in the minds of his followers in both the tragedians' and the ballad-mongers' trade was its heroine's fatal sickness: dish and clapper became attributes of this cast-out Cupid's saint, and further spots and smears were added to her beggarly costume later on. It was Henryson, then, who dealt the decisive blow to Cressid's reputation; Shakespeare's unflattering portrait of a courtesan came as a relief rather than another degradation.[1]

Recent criticism, however, has taken the edge off the traditional view of Henryson's school-masterly rigour; close reading and scholarly investigations have opened our eyes to the poem's artistic quality and to its author's humour and humanity. Cresseid, too, is seen in a more charitable light, and the *Testament* is justly called the masterpiece of Middle Scots poetry and the last flourish of a waning age.[2] In this essay I shall try to argue that the poem, if set in the tradition of Medieval and Renaissance complaint literature, may even be regarded as an attempt to correct a popular prejudice affecting the repute of a pitiable sinner.[3]

[1] For a detailed account of Cressid's literary fame see Hyder E. Rollins, 'The Troilus–Cressida Story from Chaucer to Shakespeare', *PMLA*, 32 (1917), 383–429; for ballads on her story cf. Herschel C. Baker, 'Classical Material in Broadside Ballads 1550–1625', *PMLA*, 54 (1939), 982–3.

[2] There is a concise summary of recent scholarship in the first note to Ralph Hanna's 'Cresseid's Dream and Henryson's *Testament*', in *Chaucer and Middle English Studies in Honour of Rossell Hope Robbins*, ed. Beryl Rowland (London, 1974), p. 296.

[3] I am working on a more extensive study of women's complaints in the *Heroides*—, *De claris mulieribus*—and *Mirror for Magistrates*—tradition.

The main source for the *Testament* is, of course, Chaucer's *Troilus and Criseyde*; the links are so close that for more than two centuries Henryson's 'tragedie' was taken to be a kind of epilogue to his master's tragicomic romance.[1] There is no need to run over the large number of allusions to the *Troilus*, particularly since they have been used to set Chaucer's magnanimous against Henryson's narrowminded treatment of the story so often in the past.[2] Although Chaucer had given his epic a conclusion already, there are few overlappings on a narrative level; Henryson complements rather than supplements his master's version: Chaucer had dismissed his heroine with a few regretful remarks by the middle of his last book; there are letters, but these only increase the sorrow of Troilus who dominates (if that is the word) the end of the story. Henryson will supply Cressid's end—right from the start of his account there is a shift of emphasis from Troilus, Chaucer's emotional hero, to his mistress; Chaucer tells of 'The double sorwe

[1] From William Thynne's 1532 edition of *The Workes of Geffray Chaucer* onwards and up to Chalmers' *The Works of the English Poets* (1810) the *Testament* takes its place between *Troilus and Criseyde* and *The Legend of Good Women*; Francis Thynne's *Animadversions* (1599) and Tyrwhitt's revision of the canon (1775) did little to upset this traditional order. The reasons for the attribution are open to conjecture. Thynne may have intended to make his edition more attractive by adding new material (his full title promises *Workes ... Newly Printed with Dyuers Workes whiche were Neuer in Print Before*), but this was not simply an effort to upholster an otherwise threadbare volume of poetry: Thynne's is the first one-volume-edition of Chaucer's works, on a purely commercial calculation he would rather have added a further volume to Caxton's four or Pynson's three.

If there has been an element of deceit on the part of Thynne, it was hardly noticed by his successors or their public. The language barrier was high already; Henryson's modified Middle Scots was assimilated to an equally modified Middle English which, to Dryden, sounded like 'the rude sweetness of a *Scotch* Tune' already (*Preface* to the *Fables*). No one, apparently, stumbled or only paused over Henryson's clues in the introduction where his narrator distinguishes between 'ane quair .../Writtin be worthie Chaucer glorious/ Of fair Creisseid and worthie Troylus' (40–2) and 'ane vther quair' (61), the fictitious source of the *Testament*. The Elizabethans' appreciation of Chaucer's narrative tricks and ironic twists was possibly more advanced than we care to acknowledge.

[2] See the notes in Denton Fox's excellent edition of the *Testament* (London, 1968. Quotations are taken from his text); an example of how to play off Henryson against Chaucer is given in J. S. Graydon's 'Defense of Criseyde', *PMLA*, 44 (1929), 141–77.

of Troilus' (*Tr. &Cr.*, 1, 1), Henryson of 'the fatall destenie/ Of fair Cresseid, that endit wretchitlie' (*Test.*, 62–3). The Trojan War recedes into a distance even shadier than that in Chaucer's last book. The only military action mentioned is the sally that brings Troilus to his last encounter with Cresseid.[1]

To facilitate this narrowing of focus Henryson's heroine is bereft of her contacts with both court and camp; we meet her in the privacy of her father's house and in the society of anonymous lepers. Isolation and desolation mark the last stages of her road, and she has to go it alone. Her situation is as hopeless as that of a lost maiden in Ovid's *Heroides*, in the end she is as dead to the world as a ghost from the *Mirror for Magistrates*. All she can win is her own peace of mind and our pitiful remembrance.[2]

Henryson slows down the pace of Cresseid's painful passage from court to hospital by letting his penitent pause at regular intervals for conventional expressions of her spiritual progress: there are the accusation of the gods of love, the vision of a planetary tribunal, the *ubi sunt*—lament, the formal complaint, the testament—taken together, these constitute a single flight of complaints, each step leading Cresseid further down into isolation from both gods and men.

Cresseid is not, however, entirely without support: she is given an almost invisible but omnipresent guardian in the shape of an empathetic narrator who follows her every step with concern and who strengthens her case as best he can. He adopts Cresseid's somewhat narrow view, almost regardless of the larger issues at

[1] This gives Henryson's poem—if it is allowed to take a very long view—its Alexandrian quality; the unheroic handling of incident and character may be compared to the fragmentary epics (to avoid the dubious term 'epyllion') of Catullus and Ovid, or of Tennyson and Morris. Again, Henryson follows a track laid out by his predecessor: Chaucer had already declined to sing of Troilus' deeds of arms (*Tr. &Cr.*, v, 1765–71), his emphasis was on *amor hereos*, the second part of the heroic twin formula.

Henryson's question 'Quha wait gif all that Chauceir wrait was trew?' (*Test.*, 64) I take to be no more than a playful echo of Chaucer's mocking tone. I do not think the question of authority is raised in a serious way. For a different view see Alice S. Miskimin, *The Renaissance Chaucer* (New Haven, 1975), pp. 205–8.

[2] Cresseid's isolation is mentioned time and again: 'desolait' (76), 'destitute' (92), 'clene excludit' (133), 'all forlane' (140), etc.

stake, and yet the overall perspective is not quite as restricted as that of heroines in the tradition of the *Epistolae heroides* because of this irresolutely intrusive commentator. The listener has come to know this friend a much too natural associate of Cresseid. Heroine and narrator, both servants of Venus, are linked not only by sympathy, but also by temperament: both their complexions are stricken with frost and have lost their freshness ('My faidit hart of lufe', 24,—'hir fair colour faidit', 396); their sanguine humours have dried up ('the curage doif and deid', 32,—'Thy moisture and thy heit in cald and dry', 318); their bodies are ill beyond cure; cruel Saturn, God of time and the plague, will swallow them both. The comments of this fellow sufferer are apt to affect our judgment either way.

With regard to this close affinity it is almost surprising that our narrator shows any concern with Cresseid's spiritual sickness at all, but so he does in his initial address:

> O fair Creisseid, the flour and *A per se*
> Of Troy and Grece, how was thow fortunait
> To change in filth all thy feminitie,
> And be with fleschelie lust sa maculait,
> And go amang the Greikis air and lait,
> Sa giglotlike takand thy foull plesance!
> I have pietie thow suld fall sic mischance!
>
> (78–84)

He alleviates her guilt by laying part of the blame on fortune and chance, and there is as much regret as reproach in his main charge —clad in an absolute infinitive construction that leaves out the culprit, and surrounded by compassionate exclamations—that she has miserably fallen short of his or her ideal; but the repudiation of her promiscuity or even prostitution[1] is not to be missed.

This prelude sets the tone for the tragical ballad, and it chimes in well with Chaucer's muted criticism of his hero's mistress. Chaucer, too, leaves no doubt about the irresponsibility of Criseyde's behaviour, but he also carefully avoids rubbing it in too

[1] See Denton Fox's note on the proper meaning of Cresseid's walking 'into the court, commoun' (77).

hard.[1] In a tale of courtly romance such leniency towards the notorious recreant mistress needs explanation: writing a mere 'translation', Chaucer affects obligation to his authority,

> Ne me ne list this sely womman chyde
> Forther than the storye wol devyse.
>
> (*Tr. &Cr.*, v, 1093–4)[2]

and there has been a kind of public prosecution already

> Hire name, allas! is punysshed so wide,
> That for hire gilt it oughte ynough suffise.
>
> (*Tr. &Cr.*, v, 1095–6)

Criseyde had anticipated these reactions, especially from her own sex:

> Allas! of me, unto the worldes ende,
> Shal neyther ben ywriten nor ysonge
> Na good word, for thise bokes wol me shende.
> O, rolled shal I ben on many a tonge!
> Thorughout the world my belle shal be ronge!
> And wommen moost wol haten me of alle.
> Allas, that swich a cas me sholde falle!
>
> (*Tr. &Cr.*, v, 1058–64)[3]

[1] In a careful study of sources Hans Käsmann has shown and perhaps over-emphasized Chaucer's ingenuity in almost imperceptibly making his reader aware of Criseyde's weak points. (H. Käsmann, '"I wolde excuse hire yit for routhe": Chaucers Einstellung zu Criseyde', in: *Chaucer und seine Zeit*, ed. Arno Esch (Tübingen, 1968), 97–122.)

[2] There has been no open chiding, of course, in the preceding lines; on the contrary, Criseyde has had ample opportunity of showing off contrition and of craving sympathy—an element taken from the *Roman de la rose* (and tinged with touches from Ovid's *Heroides*) rather than the *Filostrato*.

'sely', incidentally, is to become a stock epithet in pathetic women tragedies, its meaning wavering between original and modern use.

[3] The effect of this stanza depends largely upon the fact that 'Cresseid' had become a byword for infidelity even by Chaucer's time (see H. Käsmann, *op. cit.*, p. 113 'Criseydes Untreue war ja bereits sprichwörtlich geworden', and cf. Germaine Dempster, *Dramatic Irony in Chaucer*, Stanford, 1932, p. 22). There is a triple parallel to this kind of irony in the oaths of Shakespeare's Trojan protagonists (*Troilus & Cressida*, III, 2, 170–206).

In order to escape similar repercussions, Chaucer in the end refers
his female followers—in vain, as we all know—to sterner treatments of Cressid's trespasses:

> Ye may hire giltes in other bokes se
>   (*Tr. &Cr.*, v, 1776)[1]

He cannot excuse her, but neither will he accuse her.

The main cue Henryson has taken from this remarkable passage
is Criseyde's anticipation of future invective.[2] Owing to his concentration on the passions of his romantic hero Chaucer had been
unable to go beyond semi-serious compassion towards an exculpa-
tion or at least an examination of his heroine's callous behaviour.
Henryson is free from such restrictions. He will stave off Cressid's slanderers and vindicate her honour:

> Yit neuertheles, quhat euer men deme or say
> In scornefull langage of thy brukkilnes,
> I sall excuse als far furth as I may
> Thy womanheid, thy wisedome and fairnes,
> The quhilk Fortoun hes put to sic distres

[1] Guido di Colonna's widely read *Historia destructionis Troiae*, which is rather
hard on Cressid, may have inspired books of this kind (Lydgate, in one of his
rare philogynic moments, goes out of his way to soften Guido's antifeminism
by adapting an argument from *Heroides* xvi, 289–90, and making Cressid
decide a noble *bellum intestinum* between faithlessness and hard-heartedness in
favour of Diomed; *Troy Book*, iii, 4264–4448; iv, 2148–2177). Many such tracts
will have gone lost, particularly those of a more popular, satiric, or homiletic
kind (songs, pamphlets, sermons, etc.).

[2] A hundred years after the completion of *Troilus & Criseyde* Cressid's name
possibly had degenerated into a term of abuse. Chaucer's ambiguous portrait
would not have interfered with this development. His niceties were probably
lost on a century stuffed with rhetoric and romance. Nor were later generations
given to nice distinctions: many allusions in Caroline Spurgeon's collection can
be taken to refer to either Chaucer or Henryson.

Criseyde's long self-accusation (*Tr. &Cr.*, v, 1054–85) is one of Chaucer's
masterstrokes in indirect characterization. There is more than a hint of Ovid's
art in this sketch of a shallow and yet intriguing woman and her disarming,
instinctively calculated remorse. Chiding her would be in vain; indeed, the
author is wise to allow himself to be moved, perhaps amused, too, without
entering an appearance.

As hir pleisit, and nathing throw the gilt
Of the – throw wickit langage to be spilt!

(85–91)

This intention does not contradict the reproach of the preceding
stanza since it is aimed at Cresseid's reputation, not her infidelity.
Cresseid's crimes are not so gross as to justify the humiliations she
has suffered posthumously from scornful and wicked backbiters.[1]
Henryson who, throughout his writings, has shown an acute
sense in questions of justice and mercy is about to raise the problem
of fame and defamation.[2]

[1] Cautiously qualifying phrases like 'And sum men sayis' (77) and 'quhat euer
men deme or say' (85) point in a similar direction.

[2] This is a prominent motif in many complaints of forsaken, betrayed, and
fallen women throughout literary history. Ovid's coquettish Helen, e.g.,
affects apprehensions of disgrace, very much like Chaucer's Criseyde; like
Henryson's Cresseid, she would be interred rather than exposed to gossip
(*Heroides*, xvii, 207–20: *Tr. &Cr.*, v, 1054–68; *Test.*, 414–15). Chaucer's Dido
accuses Aeneas of having ruined her name:

> For thorgh yow is my name lorn,
> And alle myn actes red and songe
> Over al this lond, on every tonge.
> (*House of Fame*, 346–8)

'Shore's Wife', Churchyard's contribution to the *Mirror for Magistrates*, is driven
out of her grave by calumnious reports:

> Yea though ful dead and lowe in earth I laye,
> I heard the voyce of me what people sayd
> (*MfM*, 25, 47–8)

Daniel's Rosamond laments that no one volunteers to rescue her good name:

> *Rosamond* has little left her but her name,
> And that disgrac'd, for time hath wrong'd the same.
> . . .
> *Shores* wife is grac'd, and passes for a Saint;
> Her legend iustifies her foul attaint.
> (*Complaint of Rosamond*, 20–1, 25–6)

Shakespeare's Lucrece is driven to suicide by fear of falling prey to ballad-
mongers:

> Feast-finding minstrels tuning my defame,
> Will tie the hearers to attend each line
> (*Lucrece*, 817–18)

John Murray's Sophonisba, however, descended from a more heroic race and
age, defies the slanderous tongues of 'Lascivious Rome with her skie-mounting
towers':

Trying to do justice to his protégée Henryson not only picks up clues from his master, he also twines in threads of his own. There are marginal alterations in the minor characters: Diomed becomes a cynical seducer casting off his paramour as soon as he is weary of her company; Calchas is no longer a time-server but a quietly solicitous father; he receives his repudiated daughter with open arms—for Cresseid this kind reception must be more painful than a heap of reproaches—and he escorts his child to the spital-house in one of the most moving scenes of the poem.

Other additions like Cresseid's sickness and her last meeting with Troilus add a new dimension to the well-known story.

The question whether leprosy (or syphilis) was considered a just reward for the sin of lechery or luxury according to natural or divine laws has not yet been answered convincingly.[1] The assumption that Henryson was trying to do justice to Cresseid rather than to any abstract set of morals may offer a bypass to evade (if not a way to solve) this intricate but extraneous problem: the poem would then appear to revolve around a point of poetical rather than worldly or heavenly justice.

Cresseid's leprosy is not to be interpreted as a natural phenomenon only (a venereal disease resulting from promiscuity, nature taking revenge on one of her offenders). Apart from historical doubts (the children of Saturn, though stricken in their body, were often counted among the spiritual children of God), the structure of the poem argues against this explanation: the whole of the Olympic apparatus would be redundant. It is equally hard to believe that the planetary star-chamber is an executive body of divine justice and its verdict in keeping with a Christian

---

[1] See the dispute between Samuel Harth and R. Hanna III in *Essays in Criticism* 11 (1961), 288–97, 471–80, L. W. Patterson's learned article in *Philological Quarterly*, 52 (1973), 696–714, and D. Fox's exhaustive discussion of background material in his introduction to the *Testament*.

> Let them thus vainely prattle of my griefe,
> And mock my woes, my miseries and wrongs,
> Let them spend time in telling my mischiefe,
> Let my disgrace be subject to their songs
> (*The Tragical Death of Sophonisba*, D3ʳ)

kind of providential dispensation: these ministers of heaven are so grotesque, so sinister or lightheaded that Chaucer's famous enumeration of deities ending in 'swich rascaille!' (*Tr. &Cr.*, v, 1853) could be transferred to them.[1]

One might be tempted to assume that Henryson set up this arbitrary jury in an early-Renaissance effort to find an historical understanding of antiquity and to sound the unfathomable depths of fate in emulation of classical tragedians.[2] Cresseid's moans

> My miserie quhilk nane may comprehend,
> My frivoll fortoun, my infelicitie,
> My greit mischeif quhilk na man can amend
>
> (453-5)

would seem to support this assumption. Henryson's understanding of tragedy, however, is thoroughly medieval, and Cresseid is not as unwitting a victim as she purports to be in these exclamations—she is guilty of treacherous behaviour towards Troilus; she knows it and will accept her punishment in the end.

Nevertheless, the occasion and degree of Cresseid's chastisement are incomprehensible: the blasphemous reproaches she is charged with are well within the limits of convention; an unrequited lover's upraiding of his tutelary gods is topical in Ovidian and in Petrarchan love poetry. When Troilus hears of the plan to barter his bride for Antenor

---

[1] Henryson avoids Christian terms almost scrupulously in his *Testament*. 'God' is named only in stock phrases or in exclamations. If Henryson had intended his poem to be read allegorically he probably would have made this as clear as he did in his *Orpheus*.

[2] Blasphemies and god-sent curses are an important feature of Greek and Roman tragedies—the concept of a fate not concerned with morals did not spread, however, before the model of 'Seneca his tenne tragedies' was adopted several decades later (see Clemen's chapter on 'The dramatic lament and its forms' in his *English Tragedy before Shakespeare* (London, 1961)). The impact of this concept is felt, e.g., in Thomas Fenne's 'Hecuba's Mishaps Discoursed by Way of Apparition' (1590) when the mobled queen questions her fate with persistent poignancy and Priam reminds his wife of the curse that weighs on their line like a plague since mythic times. Here there is antique spirit in a Tudor garb.

He corseth Jove, Appollo, and ek Cupide,
He corseth Ceres, Bacus, and Cipride
(Tr. &C., V, 207–8)

and this does not provoke the wrath of the gods. Cresseid's verdict is out of proportion to both classical and courtly precedent; her earthly purgatory is more painful than the ardent but artificial griefs of *fine amour*, and yet it does not lead to fatalism or despair.

The question remains why Henryson chose to introduce this obvious incongruity of Cresseid's crime and her punishment. The answer may be that it is an advocate's triple stroke in his plea for revision of a popular misjudgment: it forestalls the prosecution's demand for a further degradation of his defendant,[1] it makes Cresseid the pitiable object of a barbarous sentence,[2] and it gives her an opportunity to suffer for her sins in this world and ask for peace in the next.[3] The trial scene, far from incriminating Cresseid,

[1] And should have prevented Henryson's followers from imputing to him a facile equation between Cresseid's dissolute life and wretched end.

[2] There is no need, of course, to accept the view of advocate or defendant who bluntly call the judges 'malitious' and 'craibit' (324, 353); even the strictest moralist in the audience, however, will have to ask himself if he can applaud this sentence.

[3] Ralph Hanna has suggested 'Cresseid's Dream' that the trial is pure phantasmagoria because it takes place in a vision of the heroine. Although one is inclined to object that this dream has horridly real after-effects for the dreamer and that Henryson is simply trying to maintain verisimilitude (Cresseid, unlike Orpheus, is an historical, not a mythic or an allegorical figure, she does not consort with the gods), there is an important point here: the scene and its agents are not seen with objective eyes—the bias, however, is the author's rather than his heroine's. Venus, e.g., is presented as hardly the right person to judge Cresseid the courtesan: her smiles are as 'Prouocatiue with blenkis amorous' (226, cf. 503) as Cresseid's used to be. Mercury, who acts as speaker in the proceedings and who by appointing the disastrous pair of Saturn and the Moon to find and to carry out Cresseid's sentence seals her fortune, is introduced in the appropriately double guise of first an orator with a touch of the minstrel (242–3), then a physician with a touch of the quack (246, 249). This ironic portrait of the patron god of liars ('With pen and ink to report all reddie, ... and not ane word culd lie'—242, 252) recalls Criseyde's apprehensions with regard to a certain kind of 'reporters', particularly since it bears likeness 'to ane poeit of the auld fassoun' (245). There may even be a smack at the master poets of the past, the red hood suggesting contemporary pictures of Dante and others (see ed. D. Fox, p. 108). Probably no personal attack is intended, but it will be remembered that Dante put Cressid into the eighth circle of his *Inferno*.

is a subtly handled means of rehabilitation—Henryson has turned an arid convention to fecund use.

Cresseid's formal complaint, a most conventional means of appealing for compassion to an audience, appears at first sight to impair rather than promote her case. With its deliberate self-incriminations it calls to mind Criseyde's parody of a love-plaint; its *ubi sunt*-catalogue, an element taken from the death-lament, points forward to the cautionary complaint of the *Mirror for Magistrates*. It is a piece of rhetorical patchwork, delivered in an importunate and impersonal manner: Cresseid almost literally takes a step beside herself, melodramatically addresses first her own person, then an imaginary assembly of ladies, and blames her miserable state on the fickleness of fortune.[1] On the face of it, this performance resembles the straining after emotional effect and the cheap moral tags of claptrap balladry that Henryson's narrator set out to counteract.[2] But Henryson's poem does not end on this note: the complaint is only Cresseid's first effort, insecure and misdirected, to come to terms with her misery. It proves a complete failure, neither consoling herself nor moving her audience. There are no ladies in the lazar-house, the rhetoric is lost on leprous outcasts, one of her fellow-sufferers calls the complainant back to bleak reality:

> Quhy spurnis thow aganis the wall
> To sla thy self and mend nathing at all?
>
> (475-6)[3]

---

[1] Clemen has analysed the topical elements of this kind of lament, self-address and *ubi sunt*-catalogue among them (*loc. cit.*).

[2] It is significant that Cresseid's rattling 'cup-and-clapper'—complaint has proved most influential on later popular treatments of her fate. This may be due to the fact, pointed out by Alice Miskimin (*op. cit.*, p. 214) that it was often separated from the *Testament* and anthologized together with Ovidian and historical poems like *The Letter of Dido to Aeneas* or *The Lament of the Duchess of Gloucester*. Unfortunately, Miss Miskimin gives no instances. To my knowledge, *The Letter of Dido* was printed only once by Pynson in his *Book of Fame* (1526), volume two of his tripartite Chaucer-edition. As to *The Lament of the Duchess*, see R. H. Robbins's comment in his *Historical Poems* (New York, 1959), pp. 344-5.

[3] The quest for consolation is another prominent motif in complaint literature. Cresseid joins Chaucer's Alcyone and Dido who also find no comfort in their plaints (*BD*, 203; *HoF*, 362-3). There are numerous examples in later poetry.

Cresseid learns to live after the law of the lepers, this eventually leads to her meeting with Troilus which brings about the recognition and redemption of her guilt in a scene totally void of rhetoric.[1] In Cresseid's last, least topical complaint compassion for Troilus is predominant and replaces former lamentations for the loss of courtly eminence. The penitent no longer blames fortune but her own faults: she herself climbed the fatal wheel, her own love was fickle and frivolous (549-52); the refrain sums up a relation that she for the first time sees in its true light:

> O fals Cresseid and trew knicht Troilus
>
> (546, 553)

Contrition marks the final stage of Cresseid's painful quest for self-knowledge. She comes to accept her fate not as the arbitrary punishment for a venial sin but as a personal act of atonement for betraying her true vocation. In the end she wins the sympathy of Troilus, her true love, and she disgraces the cruelty of her detractors.

The testament proper is free from flourishes, it soberly disposes of Cresseid's last possessions; the writer is overcome by merciful death in the middle of a sentence remembering her lover. Similarly sober and unobtrusive is the *memento mori* in the epitaph that Troilus, who feels unable to reproach his former love (601-2), sets up on her grave. The narrator's adhortation in the end is given in a subdued voice, too; his last line even approaches bathos in its laconic brevity unless it is understood to sound once more the key note of *de mortuis nil nisi bene*:

> Sen scho is deid, I speik of hir no moir
>
> (616)

---

[1] This wordless scene, so masterly contrived of glances and gestures, is Henryson's second important addition to the story and may have been one reason why he preferred a narrative form to the more dramatic monologue that seems so apt to trace the convolutions of repentance and remorse. A century later, a Scottish emulator wrote a *Last Epistle of Creseyd to Troyalus* in the true Ovidian vein.

Henryson proves to be a moralist of his own, very gentle, kind. He refuses to denounce or to condemn. He makes Cresseid suffer heavily, but he saves her from an ignominious death and he does all he can to defend her reputation against posthumous defamation. In his account of Cresseid's end he has set up an example that is designed not to deter but to encourage; without sanctifying her conduct or elevating her to the stars he reconciles Cresseid and us to her wretched fate.

The poetical justice Henryson procured for the heroine of his intensely moral but not narrowminded 'ballet schort' (610) was denied to himself for a long time, at least outside his own country. Those who attributed his poem to Chaucer appear to have winked at its beginning; those who relished his severity on Cresseid misread its ending and her testament.

V

Some Textual Problems in Donne's 'Songs and Sonets'

THEODORE REDPATH

DAME Helen Gardner's edition of the *Elegies* and *Songs and Sonets*[1] is a most notable achievement, but it would be a mistake to regard its text of the *Songs and Sonets* as definitive. We must always hope for, and work towards, establishing a still better text of these remarkable poems. The present article is an attempt to bring forward for consideration a number of cases where it is at least arguable that the text offered by Professor Gardner could be improved.

Taking cases from the poems in the order in which Professor Gardner prints them, the first case I wish to consider is from *The Message*. In line 11 *1633*[2] reads

> Which if it be taught by thine

This is altered in *1635* to

> But if it be taught by thine

which is the reading of *Lut* and *O'F*. The vast majority of MSS read 'Which'. Grierson adopted the *1635* reading 'But', and defended his decision in a note:

> It seems incredible that Donne should have written 'which if it' &c. immediately after the 'which' of the preceding line. I had thought that the *1633* printer had accidentally repeated from the line above, but the evidence of the MSS points to the mistake (if it is a mistake) being older than that. 'Which' was in the MS

[1] John Donne, *The Elegies and the Songs and Sonnets*, ed. Helen Gardner (Oxford, 1965).

[2] For lists of early editions and of MS sigla cited in this article see pp. 78–9.

used by the printer. If 'But' is not Donne's own reading or emendation it ought to be, and I am loath to injure a charming poem by pedantic adherence to authority in so small a point. *De minimis non curat lex*; but art cares very much indeed. *JC* and *P* read 'Yet since it hath learn'd by thine'.[1]

Professor Gardner, however, retains the *1633* reading 'Which'. She justifies her decision by the weight of manuscript authority:

> It is impossible, having regard to the agreement of *I, II, Dob, S96*, to regard 'But' as anything but an emendation in *Lut* to avoid the repetition that Grierson disliked. The remaining manuscripts rewrite the line to make it conform to l.3, *HK2* and *A25* showing a first stage in a process completed in *P, B, JC*.[2]

The last sentence of Professor Gardner's note refers to the reading of *HK2* and *A25*:

> Yet since there 'tis taught by thine

and the reading of *P, B,* and *JC*:

> Yet since it hath learn'd by thine

Now, is it really impossible to regard 'But' as anything but an emendation in *Lut* to avoid the repetition that Grierson disliked? Such an assertion is surely too confident? Admittedly, *I, II, Dob,* and *S96* amount to eleven reputable MSS, and one may add *DC* for good measure; but errors are often enough perpetuated in manuscript traditions, especially by faithful copyists; and 'Which' could easily have been caught from the previous line by some copyist early in the tradition. (Can we even totally rule out the possibility that it was a mistake by Donne himself in a careless moment?) Surely the question is not to be settled simply by counting pieces of paper, however respectable their authority may be? On semantic and aesthetic criteria, and possibly even on the ground

---

[1] *The Poems of John Donne*, ed. H. J. C. Grierson (Oxford, 1912), ii. 37.
[2] *Op. cit.*, p. 154.

of syntax, 'But' is here far superior to 'Which'. Grierson was entirely right; and I am glad to see that Professor A. J. Smith in his Penguin edition of Donne's poems[1] has also adopted the reading 'But'.

I want to pass now to a case in which I am making a new suggestion for the right reading in a difficult line, line 22 of *The Prohibition. 1633* reads

So shall I live thy stay, not triumph bee;

1635 altered this to

So shall I live thy Stage, not triumph be;

and the rest of the early editions followed. Grierson was not happy with the *1633* reading, and adopted *1635*'s reading 'Stage', inserting, however, commas after 'I' and 'live'. He did this 'to make quite clear that "live" is the adjective, not the verb'. He considered *1633*'s 'stay' defensible, but thought that *1633* was 'somewhat at sea about this poem', and he mentions a misprint in line 5 and some variations introduced into the text while the edition was being printed. His note continues:

> All the MSS. I have consulted support 'stage'; and this gives the best meaning: 'Alive, I shall continue to be the stage on which your victories are daily set forth; dead, I shall be but your triumph, a thing achieved once, never to be repeated'.[2]

Actually, Grierson's *apparatus criticus* cites *JC* (admittedly an inferior MS) as reading 'stay', and the Group I MSS *D*, *H49* as reading 'staye'. Moreover, in point of fact, *O'F*, which he cites as reading 'stage', looks as if it originally read 'stay', and that this was subsequently corrected to 'stage'.

Professor Gardner adopts 'Stage', but deletes the comma which Grierson had inserted after 'I', taking 'live' as a verb, cognate with 'be'. Her explanation of the line is this:

---

[1] John Donne, *The Complete English Poems* (Harmondsworth, 1971).
[2] *Op. cit.*, II. 51.

If he lives he will be the stage on which she can perpetually display her power over him instead of triumphing once and for all. The culmination of a Roman Triumph was the slaughter of the captives.[1]

Professor Gardner's critical apparatus reads as follows:

> I live,] I live *1633*: I, live, *Gr*
> Stage *Σ* [denoting 'all MSS except those specifically excepted']: stay *1633*, *H49*, *JC*.

Her apparatus is, of course, selective only, particular MSS being chosen to represent the various Groups.[2] Here, however, a fuller view of the MSS shows the following varieties of reading:

So shall I live thy staye, not triumph be
   H49, *D*; *Lut (but possibly it reads* 'stage')

So shall I live thy stay, not triumph be
   SP; *O'F (seemingly, before correction)*; *D17 (without comma)*

So shall I live thy stage, not triumph be
   O'F. (after correction); *P (without comma)*; *S962*, *B*.

So shall thy Stage, not triumph be
   Cy.

And, most important of all,

So shall I live thy stage, and triumph be
   H40

Professor Gardner does not note this reading of *H40*. The reason is, no doubt, because she does not consider *The Prohibition* to form part of the collection of Donne's poems strewn through *H40*, but takes it to be part of the miscellany found both in Harley MS 4064 and in the Rawlinson Poetical MS 31. That miscellany she desig-

---

[1] *Op. cit.*, p. 163.
[2] For the *Songs and Sonets*, these are *C57*, *H49*, and *H40*, representing Group I texts; *TCD* and *L74* representing Group II texts; *Dob*, *O'F*, and *S96*, Group III texts; and *HK2*; *Cy*, *P*; *A25*, *JC*; *B* and *S*, all V readings.

nates by the siglum $H40^\star$.[1] I am not convinced that it is correct to regard *The Prohibition* as a poem in the miscellany. It is, indeed, to be found both in Harley 4064 and *RP31*, but the text of the poem in Harley 4064 differs from that in *RP31*. I therefore submit that this poem probably was among the extra poems available to the copyist of *H40*, and should be considered as forming part of *H40* and not of *H40**. Now, Professor Gardner considers *H40* itself to offer 'the best version of the "Group I text"' of the *Songs and Sonets*. At all events I believe that the reading quoted above as that of *H40* offers an important hint towards establishing the best text of the line we are now considering. I shall attempt to justify this opinion presently. Meanwhile, however, it is worth drawing attention to the spelling 'staye' in *H49*, *D*, and possibly *Lut*. Plainly 'staye' and 'stage' could easily be mistaken for each other, either in secretary or in chancery hand. Moreover, the MS support for 'stay(e)' is at least as strong as that for 'stage'.[2]

In point of fact, 'stay' also makes much better sense in the total context of the poem than 'stage'. Stanza 1 warns the beloved not to love her lover, because the excess of joy which that would give him might kill him, and so frustrate her love for him. The second stanza warns her not to hate him, for that would kill him too, and so she would lose the glory of her triumph. The paradox therefore is that she must neither love him nor hate him, since both will kill him. Now, as is well known, the third stanza is an attempt to solve the paradox set up in the first two. 'Stage', however, would have no relevance to stanza 1, for there is no question in that stanza of the mistress wishing for 'victories' over her lover, or 'displaying her power' over him. She is imagined as *loving* him, and this love would be frustrated by his death. Contrariwise, if he were to remain alive, he would be a 'stay' for her. Similarly, in stanza 2, what she would lose by his death (which would be the result of triumphing *too much* in her victory) would be the 'style of conqueror', including, no doubt, the glory of the lover's being led alive in the triumphal procession. Stanza 3 would solve this

[1] *Op. cit.*, pp. lxv–lxvi.
[2] It is unfortunate that a number of MSS, e.g. *Lec*, *C57*, *L74*, *A25*, and *S* omit the poem; and that Group II, *DC*, *Dob*, and *S96* omit stanza 3.

paradox either in the way described in lines 19–20, or in that indicated in line 21, the result being that she will have him *both* as her 'stay' (as stanza 1 supposes she would wish) *and* as her 'triumph' (as stanza 2 supposes she would wish). I therefore propose for consideration the reading for line 22:

> So shall I live thy stay, and triumph be.

I want to pass now to another case, which also happens to be one where an interesting reading is not mentioned in Professor Gardner's edition. Line 10 of *The Indifferent* reads in *1633*, and, indeed, in all the early editions

> Will no other vice content you?

and this reading is followed by Grierson and by Professor Gardner without their noting the existence of any variant. A variant does, however, exist, and it occurs in *H40*:

> Will no other choyse content you?

'Choice' is also the reading of *Dob*, which has, however, 'vice' in the margin as an alternative or correction. It may also be worth mentioning, as possible evidence that the reading 'choice' was current in the MS tradition, that the large miscellany *S962* reads 'vice' with 'choyce' written above as an alternative or correction. Now, 'choice' has some claim, I think, to be considered the subtler reading, leaving the quip at fidelity as a 'vice' until line 12, instead of making it twice.

My next case is from *The Broken Heart*. In lines 23–4 *1633* and the rest of the early editions, and most MSS, read

> but Love, alas
> At one first blow did shiver it as glasse.

Grierson and Professor Gardner follow. There is, however, another reading in some of the MSS, namely 'one fierce', which Grierson records in his edition as the reading of the Group II MSS and of *B*. Professor Gardner does not mention this reading. Yet surely it has the advantage over 'one first' of avoiding needless and awkward redundancy? Other MSS avoid the redundancy in different ways. *S96*, for instance, reads 'At first', and the miscellany *S962* reads 'At the first'. 'Fierce', however, which is spelt 'feirce' in *A18* and *N*, is a good strong word, which accords with the violence of the explosion in stanza 1, and of the battlefield and the predatory pike in stanza 2.

Let us now turn to another case, that of line 36 in *The Will*. Here *1633* reads

Taughtst me to make, as though I gave, when I did but restore.

Grierson and Professor Gardner follow *1633*, and that reading is, indeed, supported by the great majority of the MSS; but Group III and *S* read

Taughtst me to make, as though I gave, when I do but restore.

The present tense 'do' seems to fit in better with the present tenses strewn throughout the first five stanzas of the poem. The poet *is now* restoring his reputation, industry, and so on, to their rightful owners by his will.

Let us now pass to *The Undertaking*. Two cases seem worth mentioning. The first occurs in line 16, for which *1633* and all the early editions read

Loves but their oldest clothes.

This is also the reading of *I, H40, II, D17, S,* and some other MSS, and it is adopted by Grierson (who notes, however, that *B* reads 'her'), and by Professor Gardner, who does not mention this reading. *B* is, however, not the only MS to read 'her'. *Dob* and *Lut*, which were not available to Grierson, also read 'her', and so did *O'F* before correction. The fourth of the Group III MSS, *S96*, omits this poem. Now 'her' is, I suggest, the better reading. 'Their' would most naturally refer to 'colour' and 'skin', which would make nonsense. If it were taken to refer to 'women', that would strain the syntax, and would also render the stanza needlessly obscure. The reading 'her' would refer back to 'loveliness', and the sense would be quite clear.

The second point about the text of this poem is probably less important, though worth mention. In line 25 Professor Gardner inserts a mark of elision between 'you' and 'have', printing

Then you'have done a braver thing

She says that the omission of *1633* to insert the elision mark destroyed 'a pleasing variation in the first and last stanzas'. Professor Gardner's insertion of elision marks is usually well calculated, but not so well, I think, in this particular case. The first lines of stanzas 2 to 6 are all octosyllabics. Without elision this line would be octosyllabic also. The insertion of an elision mark actually makes the line *more* like the opening line of the poem; but it also tends to take the accent *off* 'you' (where it surely ought to be?) and to put it on 'Then', where it certainly should not be. If it be argued that even with the elision mark the accent would still be on 'you', then we may ask why the elision mark should be inserted at all. There is certainly a quite pleasing enough variation in the first and last stanzas without the insertion.

I want to pass now to *A Valediction: of my name, in the window*. Space compels me to confine attention to one major point. This concerns stanza 2, which in *1633*, followed by the other early editions, reads:

'Tis much that Glasse should bee
As all confessing and through-shine as I,
'Tis more, that it shewes thee to thee,
And cleare reflects thee to thine eye.
But all such rules, loves magique can undoe,
Here you see mee, and I am you.

Grierson and Professor Gardner follow, without noting any variants in the third and fourth lines of the stanza (i.e. in lines 9 and 10 of the poem). I had always felt that 9–10 were tamely repetitive.

I was therefore glad to find, when collating MSS, that there are variants for both lines. In line 9 three of the Group III MSS (*S96, Lut,* and *O'F*) read

> 'Tis more, that it shews thee to me

though *O'F* has been corrected to the *1633* reading. In addition, the curious and not generally very reliable MS, *S*, reads 'she shewes it to me', which is of interest for the reading 'me'. The rest of the relevant extant MSS read 'thee to thee'. In line 10 the great majority of the extant MSS read 'thee to thine'; but *S96, Lut,* and *S* read 'me to thine'. *Lut,* however, has in the margin 'or/*thee* to mine', which was the reading of *O'F* before it was corrected by writing 'mee . . . thine' above, and then, subsequently, deleting 'mee', so leaving the reading of *1633*. The reading 'thee to me' in line 9 seems to me to make excellent sense, suggesting, as it does, the situation of a lover looking in from the road and seeing his mistress through the window-pane. In line 10, on the other hand, the *1633* reading seems to fit in quite well. 'Me to thine' cannot be wholly ruled out as a possibility. It could conceivably refer to the reflected glint of the scratched name. Yet, in view of lines 11–12, the more usual optical phenomenon of the reflection of the mistress's image in the pane would seem to make clearer sense. I would suggest, then, that an improvement on the *1633* text adopted by Grierson and by Professor Gardner would be

> 'Tis more, that it shewes thee to me,
> And cleare reflects thee to thine eye.

'Love's magique' then dissolves the duality of the two lovers.

A slight improvement of the text of *The Sunne Rising* is perhaps possible. In line 17 *1633* reads

> Whether both the'India's of spice and Myne

Other early editions read 'th'India's'. Neither 'the' nor 'th'' has any substantial MS support. Only two MSS out of more than a score that I have collated show an article before 'Indias' (this word itself being variously spelt, and seldom with an apostrophe). Moreover, the two MSS are *S*, which reads 'ye Indiaes' and *S962*, which reads 'the Indies', neither MS being of much authority. I suggest, therefore, eliminating the article, and pointing as in *H49*, *L74*, and *S96*:

> Whether both Indias, of spice, and mine,

The title *Lovers Infiniteness* is of some interest. This is the title in all the early editions, and Grierson retained it, though he considered it 'a strange title'.[1] It was not found in any of the MSS he had consulted, and he thought it possibly ought to be 'Loves Infiniteness', though he pointed out that 'Lovers' suits the closing thought in lines 32–3. Professor Gardner writes that 'Mon Tout' is the only title found in MS (in *A25*); and adds that, though 'the title supplied by the editor of *1633* was a good one', she accepted Grierson's suggestion 'Loves Infiniteness'. Now, actually, the title 'A Lovers Infiniteness' appears in *DC*. Moreover, *A25*'s title 'Mon Tout' also rightly suggests that it is the *capacity* for love, rather than simply love, that forms the real subject of the poem. Furthermore, since both lovers are concerned, *1633*'s title (which may, of course, have come from some lost or undiscovered MS) is an improvement on those in *DC* and *A25*. I would therefore suggest retaining *1633*'s title *Lovers Infiniteness*.

Now let us consider *A Lecture upon the Shadow*. This poem does not appear in *1633*. It was first printed in *1635*. There is interesting divergence among the MSS. The main point is that the text in Group I and *H40* differs in several places from that in Group II and *L74*. *1635* closely follows the Group II, *L74* text, except in line 26, where instead of 'first', it prints 'short', which does not occur in any known MS. Grierson follows *1635*, except in line 26; and so does Professor Gardner, with the additional exception of line 11, where she rightly adopts the *I, H40* reading 'care', in preference to 'cares'. I cannot help thinking that this adherence to the *1635* text is unwise. The Group I, *H40* readings seem to me to make a

[1] *Op. cit.*, II. 17.

more coherent poem. It is interesting, in this connection, to refer
to a statement which Professor Gardner makes in her Textual
Introduction,[1] namely, that if we are considering the possibility of
'earlier or later versions' of poems, it is possible that Group II
preserves 'earlier versions' in poems that it has in common with
$L74$, and 'later versions' in the poems that were added from an
ancestor of Group II which was not itself an ancestor of $L74$. Now,
in the poem we are considering, as I hope to show, it would be
understandable that Donne should have found the text preserved
in I and $H40$ more satisfactory than that preserved in II and $L74$,
and so have revised the latter version. The crucial differences are
in lines 9, 14, and 19. The readings for line 9 in the MSS I have
collated are

9   love I; $H40$; DC; III; $D17$, S; $S962$.
     loves II; $L74$; $A25$, P.

The balance of authority here seems to favour 'love'; but that is
not the only factor to support it. We need to consider the metaphorical structure of the poem. I suggest that in this line and in line
19 'love' is fictively embodied in the 'sun'. This is definitely
supported by the words 'westwardly decline', which most
naturally apply to the sun (cf. *The Good-morrow*, line 18: 'Without
sharp North, without declining West'). Moreover, if 'love' is the
sun in line 18, it must also be the sun in the corresponding line in
stanza 1, i.e. in line 9. This kind of interpretation is also borne
out by the reference to 'light' in line 25. Line 24 also fits in well
with this interpretation. There a contrast is drawn between 'love'
and the sun. Whereas the sun has an afternoon, and only sinks
gradually to its setting, love has no afternoon, but as soon as it
starts to decline, it is over. The 'But' which starts line 24 indicates
that up till that point the correspondence between 'love' and the
sun has been perfect. It follows that we must read 'love', not
'loves', in lines 9, 14, and 19. There is a further point in favour of
this, namely, that no provision is made in the poem for the decline
of one of the two 'loves', but not the other. The plural would

[1] *Op. cit.*, p. lxx.

therefore be irrelevant. Let us now look, however, at the MS readings for lines 14 and 19. For line 14 these are the readings for the MSS collated:

14   love *(mostly with capital 'L')* I; H40; DC; III; A25, P, D17, S; S962.
      Loves II; L74.

Here the MS evidence is very strongly in favour of the singular. For line 19 the situation is more complex:

19   If once love *(some with capital 'L')* I; H40; D17; S962.
      If Love once S.
      If our love *(with 'once' as alternative or possibly correction)* Dob.
      If our love S96 *(query capital 'L')*, Lut, O'F *(both capital 'L')*.
      If one love DC.
      If our loves II; L74; A25, P.

Here again, despite the complexity, it is clear that readings with 'love' in the singular easily outnumber those with 'love' in the plural. I suggest, then, that both on textual and on semantic grounds we should read in line 9

       So whilst our infant love did grow,

in line 14

       Except our love at this noone stay,

and in line 19

       If once love faint, and westwardly decline;

It may be worth adding that, in my view, the Group I, *H40* reading 'Those' in line 3 is slightly superior to the *1635*, II, *L74* reading 'These', because the poet is there speaking of hours which are now past. For uniformity's sake it would probably be worth accepting the Group I, *H40* readings wherever possible. This would mean reading 'which' instead of 'that' in the same line; and

'In walking' instead of 'Walking' in line 4. Semantically there is not a pin to choose between 'that' and 'which'; but 'In walking' would fit better walking to a particular place, whereas 'Walking' would fit better walking to and fro. Professor Gardner believes that the lovers must be thought of as simply strolling to and fro, with their shadows sometimes behind them, sometimes in front.[1] She calls it 'absurd' to suppose that the lovers had spent three hours walking steadily in one direction! I fail to see the absurdity. In my own youth I often walked for hours in one direction with a girl friend, and I see no reason to believe that this was impossible for a pair of lovers in the time of Donne. It seems to me that to think of the lovers as strolling to and fro, with their shadows sometimes behind them, and sometimes in front, is to miss a great mathematical beauty in the poem. As I see it, stanza 1 describes the walk of the lovers for three hours from 9 a.m. till noon, from West to East. Their shadows would fall behind them and the strange shapes would act as disguises. The lecture is then delivered at noon, when the lovers are not casting any shadows. The poet says that if their love declines from its zenith, then their shadows will fall in front of them (i.e. come from behind, or come after noon, according to whether we take 'behind' in line 17 as an adverb of place (= 'from behind') or of time (= 'later')), and this would distract them, and upset their relationship. Professor Gardner considers that 'behind' cannot be an adverb of place implying that the shadows of the first stanza which were 'before' them are now 'behind', and gives as her reason the 'absurdity' of walking for three hours in one direction, already questioned above. Even on the supposition, however, that 'behind' is an adverb of time (meaning 'later'), Professor Gardner would also need to explain 'the other way' in line 15. That expression surely must refer to place? After the noon of their love, if it started to decline, the shadows would fall 'the other way', i.e. in front of them, and would baffle the lovers themselves just as the shadows before noon had baffled others. This would happen whether they were (either actually or fictively) to continue walking from West to East, or simply stood still (either actually or fictively) facing

[1] *Op. cit.*, p. 208.

East. But to pass to another point: There is only one instance where a *1635*, Group II, *L74* reading seems superior to that of Group I, *H40*, namely in line 12, where the MS readings in the MSS I have collated are as follows:

12   the least *H49, D, Lec; H40; III; D17, S; S962.*
      the last *SP, C57.*
      the high'st *II; L74; DC ('highest'); A25.*

The fact that *SP* and *C57* both read 'the last' makes me wonder whether further back in the tradition the converse mistake of writing 'the least' for 'the last' may have occurred. 'The last' seems to make far better sense than 'the least', and just as good sense as 'the high'st'. As the extant MSS stand, however, one must, I believe, read 'the high'st'.

I want to pass now to *The Dreame*. Professor Gardner's text of this poem has been sharply criticized by several scholars and critics.[1] Controversy has largely centred around lines 19–20, but several other lines deserve consideration. I am inclined to think that Professor Gardner is right in reading in line 7

Thou art so true, . . .

I was so strongly impressed by Grierson's note[2] on that line that I read 'truth' in my own edition of the *Songs and Sonets*;[3] but I have searched in vain for a parallel use of 'so' to qualify a noun. I think it probable, as Professor Gardner suggests,[4] that 'truth' may have been caught from the line below. With regard to line 8, she may also be right in considering it more probable that the original reading was 'truth' and that 'truths' arose independently in *L74, TCC, O'F, HK2*, etc., from attraction to the other plurals in the line, than that 'truth' was caught from the line above; since

[1] Mark Roberts, review of H. Gardner's Edition, *Essays in Criticism*, 16 (1966), 309–29; and *Essays in Criticism*, 17 (1967), 263–77, at pp. 271–2; William Empson, *Critical Quarterly*, 8 (1966), 255–80, at pp. 266–9; J. C. Maxwell, *Modern Language Review*, 61 (1966), 275–8, at p. 276.

[2] *Op. cit.*, II. 33–4.

[3] *The Songs and Sonets of John Donne*, ed. T. Redpath (London 1956).

[4] *Op. cit.*, p. 209.

Lut, S96 read 'truth' in line 8, although they read 'true' in line 7. Another crux occurs, of course, in line 14. *1633–1719* read

> (For thou lovest [*or* 'lov'st'] truth) an Angell, at first sight,

and Grierson and Professor Gardner follow. The MS evidence is interesting:

> (Thou lov'st [*or* 'lovest'] truth) but an Angell, at first sight, *I; II; L74; DC.*
> (For thou lov'st truth) an ... *III; Cy, P, S; S962.*
> (For thou louest truthes) An ... *A25.*

Professor Gardner argues against the reading of Groups I and II that 'but' here and 'But' at the start of line 15 would be awkward; and also that the reading makes the point of the divine attribute of of the mistress too early, spoiling 'the fine hyperbole of the close'. These are certainly arguments that deserve consideration; but I do not find them altogether convincing. The presence of 'but' in the highly authoritative MSS in which it appears needs explaining; and Professor Gardner's suggestion that it may have been inserted to fill out the line after a loss of the initial 'For' through the opening bracket in some MS being carelessly made, and seeming to cancel the word, though possible, does not seem overwhelmingly plausible. The mistake, being common to Groups I and II, must have occurred at least as far back as their common ancestor, the MS*a* (if we accept Professor Gardner's stemma[1]), and, since this MS would also be the ancestor of the MSS that read 'For', and do not read 'but', it would be most strange that somewhere in the transmission from *a* to them a copyist or other person should have hit upon the idea of deleting 'but' and inserting 'For' within the brackets. An alternative hypothesis to explain the divergence between the readings would be that somewhere in the separate lines of transmission to Group I, Group II, and *L74*, the same mistake resulting in the reading '(Thou lov'st truth) but an Angell, at first sight' should have been made; but this is also extremely hard to believe. We are left then with two possibilities: (1) that *a* itself

---

[1] *Op. cit.*, p. lxxviii.

(the common ancestor of all the MSS) contained the word 'For' and a bracket which to some copyists looked as if it cancelled the word, and to others did not; or (2) that Donne revised the reading one way or the other, and informed some of his friends accordingly. Of these two possible explanations I find (2) the more credible, though (1) is not impossible. The question then would be: Which was the revision? Professor Gardner suggests that the Group III MSS are further from Donne's papers than the MSS of Groups I and II. On the other hand, *1633* reads 'For though lovest truth'. The point is a hard one. The editor of *1633* may have been baffled (or embarrassed) by the reading in his Group I and Group II MSS, and have had recourse in this case to a Group III MS for that reason. On textual grounds I would assess the claims of Groups I and II here as somewhat superior to those of Group III, though perhaps not much. The aesthetic factors, in such a case, might be decisive. Professor Gardner's point about the two 'buts' does not seem to me a strong one. There is a not dissimilar proximity of 'buts' in lines 23–4 of *A Lecture upon the Shadow*; and in line 17 of *The Anniversarie*. As to her point about revealing the great secret too early, I suggest that the reading '(Thou lov'st truth) but an Angell, at first sight', is not only itself a wittier line (as Professor Gardner admits) but an intriguing one, which, as the poem unrolls, leads up to the climax without immediately suggesting its full definition.

It is time now, however, to broach the problem of lines 19–20. In *1633* these read

> I must confesse, it could not chuse but bee
> Prophane, to thinke thee any thing but thee.

and *1635–1719* followed, and so did Grierson. The extant MSS, however, read 'I doe confesse', and Professor Gardner emends *1633* accordingly. It would be interesting to know where the *1633* editor got 'must' from; but with the present MS evidence, it is certainly right to read 'do'. For the remainder of the two lines, Professor Gardner follows *1633*. MS readings are as follows:

19 I *A25, Cy, P, S; S962. (Evidently also HK2, B)* it *I; II; L74; DC; III.*

20 Profanenes *or* Prophannes *or* Prophanenes(se) *I; II; L74; DC; S96, Dob.*
Profane *or* Prophane *Lut;*[1] *A25, Cy, P, S. O'F also finally reads 'Profane', apparently after being corrected twice, from 'Profane' to 'Profanesse', and back again.*

Professor Gardner writes:

I reject 'Prophaness', in spite of its high manuscript authority, because I can find no parallel in Donne's lyric verse for a line with an extra syllable attached to its first foot with no possibility of an elision. 'Prophaness' gives a hopelessly unmetrical line and ruins the splendid run of the stanza up to its climax. I cannot believe that Donne wrote it, and prefer the charge of inconsistency to that of being deaf to the music of Donne's verse.[2]

Now, in point of fact, there seem to be a number of lines in the *Songs and Sonets* with an extra syllable attached to the first foot with no possibility of an elision. If any one of the following lines is of such a kind, Professor Gardner's generalization is invalid:[3]

Who e'r rigg'd/faire ship/to lie/in harbors,
(*Confined Love*, 15)

By being/to thee/then what/to me/thou wast;
(*The Prohibition*, 5)

As virtu/ous men/pass mild/ly away,
(*A Valediction: forbidding mourning*, 1)

---

[1] Professor Gardner says that Group III reads 'Prophaness'. This is not the case. One Group III MS, *Lut*, reads 'Prophane'. Incidentally, it is curious that, as Professor Empson pointed out in his review of the edition (*art. cit.*, 268), Professor Gardner does not indicate in her critical apparatus (p. 80) which other MSS read 'Prophane'. She merely refers, in her Notes (p. 210), to 'MSS outside the main groups'.

[2] *Op. cit.*, p. 210.

[3] I indicate what would seem a reasonable scansion in each case.

On man hea/vens infl/uence workes/not so

(*The Extasie*, 57)

And burde/nous cor/pulence/my love/had growne,

(*Loves Diet*, 2)

These are not the only cases, but they should suffice. It is possibly worth adding the line from *The Dreame* with scansion marks to indicate the possible parallels:

Profaneness,/to thinke/thee an/y thing/but thee.

It might be objected against some of the examples I have given that the first foot is really an iambus, and the second an anapaest. If that mode of scansion were adopted for my examples, however, precisely the same scansion would apply to the line from *The Dreame*. Therefore, I suggest, Professor Gardner's generalization does not hold. There remains, however, the aesthetic issue. Is this line with 'Profaneness' really 'hopelessly unmetrical'? If any one of my examples is a true parallel, it also will be 'hopelessly unmetrical', yet Professor Gardner has printed all those other lines without demur. My own view is that none of them is hopelessly unmetrical, and I find myself in good company in thinking that the reading of Groups I and II in line 20 of *The Dreame* is rhythmically quite acceptable. Mr. J. C. Maxwell, in his review of Professor Gardner's edition,[1] found nothing objectionable in the reading 'Profanes', and Professor Mark Roberts not only thought that there were insufficient grounds for rejecting that reading but also reported that Mr. F. W. Bateson had told him in a letter that he actually preferred the reading 'on prosodic grounds'.[2] There is, however, a point against reading 'Profaneness' (in any of its spellings) which Professor Gardner does not mention, namely, that the ending could easily have been caught from 'confess(e)' in the preceding line. I do not, however, think that that objection has enough weight to overcome the strong MS evidence for 'Pro-

[1] *Art. cit.*, 276.
[2] *Essays in Criticism*, 17 (1967), 277.

faneness'. It is worth while now to consider the evidence for reading 'I' instead of 'it' in line 19. It is important to note that the MS readings suggest that two versions were current before the publication of *1633*:

> I doe confesse, I could not chuse but bee
> Prophane, to thinke thee any thing but thee.

and

> I doe confesse, it could not chuse but bee
> Prophaness, to think thee any thing but thee.

We have no reason to believe that there was any substantial MS support for the *1633* version adopted by Grierson and by Professor Gardner. Of the two versions for which there is substantial MS support I would suppose that the version 'I . . . Prophane' is the earlier, and I would guess that Professor Empson[1] was quite possibly right in suggesting that Donne altered the line when revising his poem, so as not to confess that he was profane. If Professor Gardner is right in thinking that Group I MSS descend from a revised text of 1614, just before Donne's ordination, Professor Empson's suggestion would seem to have considerable probability. Which version, then, it may be asked, should a modern editor print? If he has to print one and only one in his text, I believe he should perhaps print the more vital version 'I . . . Prophane'; but he should also make it abundantly clear that there was another version, and should print it somewhere on the same or on a facing page. In any case, he should not print the bastard version of *1633*.

I now want to turn to two cases in *Twicknam Garden*—not, however, the case of 'nor leave this garden' in line 15, which I had already adopted in my own edition in 1956. The first case for present discussion is in line 2. It is not of major importance, but it involves a variant of some interest not recorded either by Grierson or by Professor Gardner. *1633–1719* read

> Hither I come to seeke the spring,

[1] *Art. cit.*, 268.

and this reading is followed both by Grierson and by Professor Gardner. The MSS I have cited here, however, are divided, some reading 'came':

2   come *I; H40; DC; III; Cy, P, S; S962.*
    came *II; L74; A25, D17.*

The weight of MS authority is on the side of 'come'; but 'came' is an interesting reading, fully worth consideration. Aesthetically it has advantages. 'Hither I come' has the air of an announcement of an actor's entry, which ill assorts with the mood of bitter desperation conveyed in the stanza as a whole. Semantically also, the distinction of tense from the present of 'I do bring' gives perspective to the disillusion. I should not want to press these claims of 'came' very strongly, but it seems to be a reading at least worth mention.

The other case occurs in line 17, and it has already evoked comment.[1] *1633* reads in lines 17–18

> Make me a mandrake, so I may grow here,
> Or a stone fountaine weeping out my yeare.

Grierson emended 'grow' to 'groane' on MS evidence, commenting

> It is surely much more in Donne's style than the colourless and pointless 'growe'. It is, too, in closer touch with the next line. If 'growing' is all we are to have predicated to the mandrake, then it should be sufficient for the fountain to 'stand', or 'flow'. The chief difficulty in accepting the MS reading is that the mandrake is most often said to shriek, sometimes to howl, not to groan.[2]

Nevertheless, he argues that the lover most often groans, and that in a metaphor where two objects are identified such a transference of attributes is quite permissible, and quotes *2 Hen. VI*, III.ii. 310–11, in which the mandrake is actually said to 'groan':

[1] e.g. by Professor Mark Roberts in *Essays in Criticism*, 16 (1966), 315–16.
[2] *Op. cit.*, II. 26.

Would curses kill, as doth the mandrake's groan,
I would invent as bitter searching terms, &c.

He also adds lines 53–4 of Donne's *Elegie upon . . . Prince Henry*:

> though such a life wee have
> As but so many mandrakes on his grave.

with the comment: 'i.e. a life of groans'. Professor Gardner restores the *1633* reading. Her note reads:

> I differ from Grierson in retaining the reading of *1633* which follows *C57* and *Lec* against the other Group I manuscripts and Group II. As a general rule I have abandoned *1633* on such occasions; but here *C57* and *Lec* have the support of Group III and *HK2*, &c. 'Groane', the reading of Groups I and II, could have arisen independently from the strong association of mandrakes with groans. But the mandrake was not held to groan when *in situ*; it only groaned when it was torn up; see Browne, *Pseudodoxia Epidemica*, book ii, chap. vi.[1]

Professor George Williamson had already defended 'grow', as more closely associated with 'senseless' and 'mandrake', all three representing the 'vegetal' soul, which was below the 'sensible' soul, and entirely incapable of sensation.[2] The crux is not an easy one. 'Groan' is a more exciting word, and links more clearly with line 18. It is also emotionally more in tone with the rest of the poem. Yet 'grow' is not as pointless as Grierson thought. If 'grow' were accepted, 'so' should probably be taken to mean 'as long as', or 'if only'; whereas, with the reading 'groan' it would probably mean 'so that', though it could have the other meaning. The readings of the MSS cited in this article are:

17 gro(a)ne *H49, D, SP; H40; DC; TCC, A18, N, TCD* (*which was first altered from* 'groane' *to* 'growe', *and then back again to* 'groane').
grow(e) *Lec, C57; L74; III; A25, Cy, P, D17, S; S962.*

---

[1] *Op. cit.*, p. 216.
[2] 'Textual Difficulties in Donne's Poetry', *Modern Philology*, 38 (1940), repr. in *Seventeenth Century Concepts* (London, 1960).

As Grierson observed, the spellings 'grone' and 'growe' could easily be mistaken for each other. It seems to me, then, that the MS evidence is inconclusive. We must therefore hope to settle the point by other criteria. Professor Gardner's strictures about the occasions on which mandrakes were held to groan is countered by the Donne passage quoted by Grierson. Poets cannot be expected to observe the precise limits of scientific truth. On semantic and aesthetic criteria I believe 'groan' is to be preferred. I am glad to see that Professor Smith has chosen to read 'groan' in his Penguin edition of Donne's Poems.

This ends my discussion. The cases I have considered are not the only ones where I think improvements could be made. They are simply those on which I have felt ready to say something which I hope may be useful.

EARLY EDITIONS OF DONNE'S POEMS CITED IN THIS ARTICLE
1633, 1635, 1639, 1650, 1654, 1669, 1719.

MS SIGLA OF MSS COLLATED AND CITED IN THIS ARTICLE
MSS containing collections of Donne's poems (I am adopting the group nomenclature initiated by Grierson and amended by Professor Gardner).

Group I (H49, D, SP, Lec, C57)

H49 British Museum, Harleian MS 4955.
D Dowden MS, Bodleian Library, MS Eng. Poet. e 99.
SP St. Paul's Cathedral Library, MS 49 B 43.
Lec Leconfield MS (in the library of Sir Geoffrey Keynes).
C57 Cambridge University Library, Add. MS 5778.

H40 British Museum, Harleian MS 4064.

Group II (TCC, A18, TCD, N)

TCC Trinity College, Cambridge, MS R 3 12.
A18 British Museum, Add. MS 18647.

TCD Trinity College, Dublin, MS G 2 21.

N Norton MS, Harvard College Library, MS Eng. 966/3.

L74 British Museum, Lansdowne MS 740.

DC Dolau Cothi MS, National Library of Wales.

Group III (S96, Dob, Lut, O'F)

S96 British Museum, Stowe MS 961.
Dob Dobell MS, Harvard College Library, MS Eng. 966/4.
Lut Luttrell MS (in the library of Sir Geoffrey Keynes).
O'F O'Flaherty MS, Harvard College Library, MS Eng. 966-5.

MSS outside Groups I–III (called V by Prof. Gardner)

Cy Carnaby MS, Harvard College Library, MS Eng. 966/1.
P Phillipps MS, Bodleian Library, MS Eng. Poet. f 9.
A25 British Museum, Add. MS 25707.
D17 Victoria and Albert Museum, Dyce Collection, MS D25 F17.
S Stephens MS, Harvard College Library, MS Eng. 966/6.

Note: Five other extant MSS containing collections of Donne's poems, and cited by Professor Gardner, I have not collated for this article. These are: *HK2* (Haslewood-Kingsborough MS, 2nd part), *O* (Osborn MS), *JC* (John Cave MS) (of which, however, *D17*, which I have collated, is known to be a duplicate), *B* (Bridgewater MS), *K* (King MS). I should be very surprised, however, from what I know of these MSS, if they were to entail any modification of the conclusions I have reached in this article.

MS Miscellanies containing poems by Donne
   H40* British Museum, Harleian MS 4064.
   RP31 Bodleian Library, Rawlinson Poetical MS 31.
   S962 British Museum, Stowe MS 962.

VI

'The Changeling' and the Drama of Domestic Life

LEO SALINGAR

IN one of the earliest of critical allusions to Middleton, Leigh Hunt observed that 'there is one character of his (De Flores in *The Changeling*) which, for effect at once tragical, probable, and poetical, surpasses anything I know of in the drama of domestic life'.[1] The terms of Leigh Hunt's praise were happily chosen, especially if in his brief classification he meant to distinguish *drama* from *tragedy*. For *The Changeling* is a serious, exciting play, a drama of strongly tragical cast, without quite attaining that plenary combination of emotional intensity with imaginative range for which *tragedy* would be the only appropriate description. It is a tragedy in form, of course, but not in the full possible effect. And its limitations, together with its special kind of intensity, appear to spring from its concentration upon domestic life as its subject.

Although *The Changeling* and *Women Beware Women* were by far the outstanding achievements of the London theatres in the later years of James I, and quite distinctive in their point of view, they were typical of the day in the kind of subject-matter they offered. 'Our pulpits,' wrote John Chamberlain the news-reporter early in 1620, 'ring continually of the insolence and impudence of women' (he had already noted that the campaign had been orchestrated from the throne), 'and to helpe the matter forward the players have likewise taken them to taske, and so to the ballades and ballad-singers, so that they can come nowhere but

---

[1] *Imagination and Fancy* (1844), quoted, N. W. Bawcutt, ed., *The Changeling* (London, 1958), p. xlv (quotations from the play are taken from this edition).

theyre eares tingle.'[1] As far as plays are concerned, in one sense
Chamberlain exaggerates, since they were at least as likely to
defend or idealize women as to denounce them; but he hardly
exaggerates the interest taken in feminine morals—an interest
advertised by such titles, from the years about 1619–20, as *All's
Lost by Lust, The Fatal Dowry, The Double Marriage,* or *The Virgin
Martyr.* All these were nominally tragedies; and most nominal
tragedies of the day still kept the convention that their leading
characters were of princely rank or near it. But whereas early in
the reign tragic stories of domestic passion had been intermingled
with 'state-affairs' (as in *Othello* or *Bussy D'Ambois*), 'state-affairs'
now amounted to no more than a background or a dramatic
pretext for a sexual intrigue; and *The Duchess of Malfi* (*c.* 1614) was
the last play for many years to connect private and political
morality in anything approaching an inclusive tragic vision.
Meanwhile, comedy was losing satiric drive and the enjoyment of
hard-headed intrigue in favour of tragicomedy in Fletcher's
manner. The contrast between Middleton's *A Trick to Catch the
Old One* (*c.* 1605) and Massinger's *A New Way to Pay Old Debts*
(*c.* 1625) typifies two generations; although Massinger takes over
the essentials of Middleton's plot, he turns it almost into a tract.
He is not more observant than Middleton about social behaviour
and class distinctions, but he is much more in earnest, creating a
Fletcherian melodrama rather than a comedy of intrigue. Nevertheless, Fletcher's style of playwriting was not the only style,
influential as it was. A number of serious plays of the period, such
as *A Fair Quarrel, The Witch of Edmonton* and *The English Traveller,*
are neither tragedies *manqués* nor Fletcherian bravura pieces
(though they are classified as 'tragicomedy'). Nor again, though
their subject-matter is domestic, are they simply didactic, like
Heywood's earlier *A Woman Killed with Kindness.* At their best,
these plays present, in the form of a dilemma rather than a sermon,
topical problems of social life—the duelling code, the persecution
of witches, incompatible marriages. They hardly constitute
between them a new and distinct genre in the theatre, but they

[1] Letters of January 25 and February 12, 1620, quoted, Louis B. Wright,
Middle-class Culture in Elizabethan England (Chapel Hill, 1935), p. 493.

already contain some of the main ingredients of the *drame bour-geois* and the problem play of the eighteenth and nineteenth centuries. And they bring out the dominant concern of the theatres in the years round about 1620 with middle- and upper-class family life.

Two factors in particular help to account for this trend. One was the contraction of the national, miscellaneous theatre-going public of Shakespeare's day, and the consequently increased preponderance of the leisure-class audiences in the private play-houses in London. The other was the strain on the position of the gentry, made manifest by the aggressive mood of the Parliament that assembled in 1621, which brought about the downfall of Buckingham's kinsman, Mompesson, and the impeachment of Lord Chancellor Bacon.[1] Parliament was alarmed by the trading depression and the king's foreign policy, but there were also more widespread causes for disquiet. On one side, the gentry were hereditary landowners and potential servants of the Crown: 'Gentlemen are *nobiles inferiores*', as Coke reminded the Commons in 1621, 'the Lords are but *nobiles superiores*'.[2] But honours were cheapened by the sale of titles, preferment at court was blocked by Buckingham's clan, and the king's leaning towards Spain appeared to threaten religion while denying to the aristocracy their tradi-tional aspiration to profits and glory from war (nostalgia for military honour is a frequent theme with Fletcher's and Massinger's heroes). On the other side, the landed gentry were both rivals and allies to the merchants of the City. If they were often their debtors, they were also their business associates, eager to share in a 'free trade', and allied to them by marriage (it is significant that both in *A Trick to Catch the Old One* and in *A New Way to Pay Old Debts* the grasping City man is no stranger to the young heir, but his uncle); moreover, their whole style of living took them increasingly away from their country estates into Lon-don. For many, therefore, their actual position in society was at variance with their theoretical rôle. They resisted when the king

[1] Cf. Robert Zaller, *The Parliament of 1621* (Berkeley, 1971).
[2] W. Notestein, F. H. Rolf and H. Simpson, eds., *Commons Debates, 1621* (New Haven and London, 1935), III, p. 21.

tried to force them back to their duties as county magistrates at a time of economic unrest; but even a parliamentary oppositionist like Sir James Parrot could agree with the king in 1621 that one of the principal causes of 'the present decaie and weaknes of the Kingdome' was 'the prodigallitye of the Gentrie by bringing their wives soe much to London'.[1] Moral indignation over women's dress and behaviour was another aspect of the same complaint. Nevertheless, a cool observer could see that mere anti-feminism dealt at most with the symptoms of a social malaise and not its underlying causes; in the letter where Chamberlain reports the king's instructions to preachers in 1620 'to inveigh vehemently against the insolencie of our women' he adds that 'the truth is the world is very much out of order, but whether this will mende it God knowes'.[2] On the stage, what was virtually a debate over the honour of women was only part of a wider questioning or re-affirming of the general idea of honour, as the conceptual basis and justification of the social status of the gentry.

For a traditional theorist like Henry Peacham, genuine honour, as distinct from a purchased title, was 'the reward of Virtue and glorious Actions onely', but the 'Honour of blood' in a true noble or gentleman was 'innate', 'inherent and Naturall' like the lustre of a 'Diamond', infixed in 'the Frame of the whole Universe'[3] and commanding social privilege, including privileged treatment by the law.[4] Massinger upholds a similar conception, in spite of or even because of the irrationalities it involves. For example, in *The Fatal Dowry* (written in collaboration with Nathan Field, *c.* 1619), he pits the inherited military honour of young Charalois against the mercenary and frivolous values of the city, and finally against the levelling tendencies of the law. Rewarded with the gift of a wealthy bride for the self-sacrifice he has undertaken in order to redeem his dead father's reputation, Charalois then finds his wife in adultery with the city upstart, young Novall. He kills them both, like a Spanish vindicator of the *pundonor*. His father-in-

[1] *Commons Debates* IV, pp. 436–7.
[2] Wright, *loc. cit.*
[3] *The Compleat Gentleman* (1622: ed. G. S. Gordon, 1906), pp. 1–3.
[4] Ibid., p. 13.

law, an upright justice, is torn between moral approval and his feelings as a father. In the closing scene, before a hostile public court, Charalois is acquitted for his integrity, 'notwithstanding you have gone beyond/The letter of the law'—though at the last moment he is murdered by a partisan of young Novall in an act of private revenge. In this way the dramatists suggest an uneasy compromise between the mystique of honour and the doctrine of retribution. But the main function of the tragic business in plays like this is to exalt the ideal of honour by submitting it to extravagant tests.

Middleton's attitude is entirely different (or the attitude he shares with Rowley in their close collaboration in *The Changeling* (1622)). The realism he is often praised for is partly a matter of creating an impression of credible surroundings from common life, and partly a matter of mental scale; he measures extravagance in his characters' thoughts by tacit comparison with the normal. This in turn has much to do with his unusual psychological penetration, his gift for exposing velleities and self-deception in his characters. Above all, Middleton's realism is a quality of moral judgment, an insistence on the unavoidable. 'Can you weep fate from its determin'd purpose?'—the terrible resonance of this line comes, not from De Flores's brutal self-assertion, and still less from any hint of an external destiny, but from the revelation of a natural force. 'Lust and forgetfulness has been amongst us', Hippolito exclaims, towards the end of *Women Beware Women*: the tragic shock for Middleton's characters is the recognition of moral facts they have always known, but have induced themselves to forget.

Middleton's realism includes social as well as psychological insight. In his best plays he sketches out a social community, however divided within itself, and the comic or tragic aberrations of his leading characters are aberrations that social intercourse permits, encourages or fosters.[1] In this respect he stands at the

---

[1] Cf. Inga-Stina Ewbank, 'Realism and Morality in *Women Beware Women*', *Essays and Studies 1969*. (I have gained much from the discussion of Middleton's social and political connections in the draft of a forthcoming book by Margot Heinemann.)

opposite pole to a dramatist like Massinger. Social standards in his plays are created by men, not for them; honour is not an absolute but a social convention. More than that, it can become a dangerous illusion, an instrument of self-destruction. What finally betrays Beatrice Joanna is precisely the confidence in her birth and status that she has absorbed from the society around her. And *The Changeling* is not merely a character-portrait of a perverse young woman, but a study in what can fairly be called class-consciousness.

A distinctive note in his characters is the homely way they usually express their feelings, with little of that grandeur so often assumed in earlier Jacobean tragedies. In *The Changeling*, Alsemero —the traveller, as we soon learn—thinks of marriage as his natural 'home', man's 'right home back, if he achieve it' (I.i.9); Beatrice thinks of her 'joys and comforts' (II.i.96; II.ii.32); De Flores demands to be 'eas'd' of his passion, and promises Beatrice 'peace' when she surrenders (III.iv.99, 169). Their inward goal, it seems, is commonplace tranquillity. And their language is charged with allusions to religion, in phrases like 'I keep the same church', 'I shall change my saint', 'Requests that holy prayers ascend heaven for', or 'heaven has married her to joys eternal'. These phrases come from scenes that have been attributed separately to Rowley and to Middleton,[1] and their similarity shows how closely the two writers must have worked together. But they belong in any case to the common idiom of the time. Except for Alsemero's opening soliloquy, the characters are not thinking deliberately about religion, but (with whatever unconscious irony) using religious phrases casually and unreflectingly, for the sake of affirmation. Theirs is a religion of convention, part of their feeling of security in their world.

Yet a hint of insecurity is sounded from the outset, as Alsemero questions his own impulse:

> 'Twas in the temple where I first beheld her,
> And now again the same; what omen yet
> Follows of that? None but imaginary;

---

[1] I.i.35, 155 (attributed to Rowley); II.ii.9, III.iv.5. See Bawcutt, p. xxxix.

Why should my hopes or fate be timorous?
The place is holy, so is my intent.

He voices a doubt only to suppress it, but for insufficient reason, relying illogically on the building, 'the temple'. So too Vermandero counts on the security of his castle, the principal 'place' in the drama, when he cautiously extends a welcome to Alsemero:

> I must know
> Your country; we use not to give survey
> Of our chief strengths to strangers; our citadels
> Are plac'd conspicuous to outward view,
> On promonts' tops; but within are secrets.
>
> (I.i.162)

Vermandero commands 'a most spacious and impregnable fort' (III.i.4), in which however the 'secrets' are hidden from his own knowledge, in the retired rooms where lovers but also eavesdroppers can meet and in the 'narrow' stairways and dark corridors where Alonzo and then Diaphanta can be lured to their deaths. It has a moral as well as a physical existence in the play.[1] It stands for the 'labyrinth' where Beatrice loses herself (III.iv.71). And in the shock of the last scene a glimpse of this double meaning rushes into her father's unsuspecting mind: 'An host of enemies enter'd my citadel/ Could not amaze like this' (v.iii.147). In military terms the 'secrets' provide the 'strengths' of the fortress, but in moral terms it is the apparent 'strengths' that make possible the 'secrets'.

Both Alsemero and Beatrice lay great store by rational 'judgment' (again, in speeches probably written by each of the dramatists).[2] But like the citadel, 'judgment' gives a false sense of security, hiding and sanctioning irrational desires. Again and again in the early scenes the characters show themselves headstrong or petulant or attribute to others disturbed feelings that evidently belong to themselves. Alsemero, the reasoner, is the first in the play to

[1] Cf. T. B. Tomlinson, *A Study of Elizabethan and Jacobean Tragedy* (Cambridge and Melbourne, 1964), pp. 204–5.

[2] E.g. I.i.16, 72–9; and II.i.7, 13.

'change' (i.i.34), but when Jasperino asks him 'What might be the cause?', his retort seems more a reflex of his own mood than of anything in his friend's question: 'Lord, how violent/Thou art!' (i.i.40). There is no apparent provocation for Beatrice's rage against De Flores, and Alsemero can only explain it away as 'a frequent frailty in our nature'—without considering how far, in the end, his explanation may stretch (i.i.93–128). Jasperino calls himself a 'mad wag' in his flirtation with Diaphanta, giving occasion for the first mention of the madhouse in the sub-plot. In one of the many asides of the play, emphasizing the contrast between professed and intimate feelings, Beatrice admits to herself 'a giddy turning' in her affections (i.i.156); and when Vermandero announces that Alonzo is 'hot preparing' for the wedding, she accuses her father of being 'violent', much as Alsemero had accused Jasperino (i.i.189–91). This leads on to a three-part refrain about 'will': 'I'll want/ My will else', says Vermandero about the marriage he has planned; Beatrice rejoins in an aside, 'I shall want mine if you do it'; and after the short though significant incident with her gloves, De Flores, alone, brings the scene to an end with

> No matter, if but to vex her, I'll haunt her still;
> Though I get nothing else, I'll have my will.

By this point the word 'will' has clearly taken on its secondary meaning of sexual desire,[1] but the more general sense is still predominant. Vermandero is the brusque, affable commandant, fond of his only daughter but remote from her (as Brabantio had been remote from Desdemona). He is a man of duty, but, as he shows later, when Tomazo comes to claim justice from him (iv.ii), his self-regarding 'honour', with its strain of authoritative bluster, comes first. In the opening scene, he overbears Alsemero, good-naturedly enough but obstinately, when the latter—for the second time in the play—changes his mind: 'How, sir? By no means;/ ... You must see my castle,/ ... I shall think myself unkindly us'd else' (i.i.200–203). And in the same strain he goes

[1] Christopher Ricks, 'The Moral and Poetic Structure of The Changeling', Essays in Criticism, 10 (1960), 294.

on to boast of the match he has arranged: 'I tell you, sir, the gentleman's complete,/ . . . I would not change him for a son-in-law/ For any he in Spain . . .'—and so on, with a sting of sarcasm when Alsemero can only offer him a minimally polite congratulation:

Als.   He's much
    Bound to you, sir.
Ver.   He shall be bound to me,
    As fast as this tie [Beatrice] can hold him; I'll want
    My will else.
                                    (I.i.212–19)

Both of the men are embarrassed, for reasons that have nothing to do with the overt course of their conversation; what troubles Vermandero is any challenge to his authority, particularly from his own daughter. The context, then, of the word 'will' here is a struggle within the family, and this gives the plain sense that Beatrice intends in her aside. Even when De Flores repeats the word with a perceptible sexual overtone, his chief meaning is not that he expects to 'have [his] will' of Beatrice in the sense of raping her, but that he is determined to 'haunt her still', 'if but' (no more than) 'to vex her'; he 'cannot choose but love her', but he refuses to be humiliated by her contempt. The guiding thread throughout the long opening scene is wilfulness, self-assertion as opposed to 'judgment'. Similarly, Alonzo will brush aside his brother's warning that Beatrice's 'dulness' towards him bodes ill for his 'peace' if he persists in marrying her. 'Why, here is love's tame madness' is Tomazo's comment; and, echoing the word De Flores had applied to Beatrice, 'thus a man/ Quickly steals into his vexation' (II.i.124–55). The point is not that Alonzo is exceptionally passionate, but that he has disregarded the plain evidence in front of him, rather than admit that he has made a mistake.

Beatrice is the second character in the play to change. No sooner has she delivered her sage if coquettish admonition to her fresh suitor about 'judgment' and 'rashness' than she wishes, in her first aside,

For five days past
To be recall'd! Sure, mine eyes were mistaken . . .
(I.i.84)

She can lie to herself as well as to others, and her revulsion from
De Flores—who believes that 'she knows no cause for't but a
peevish will' (I.i.107)—represses a kind of fascination. So much is
apparent when, at the end of the opening scene, she furiously
throws down her glove as if to challenge or provoke him. In their
second meeting on the stage, 'This ominous ill-fac'd fellow more
disturbs me/ Than all my other passions' (II.ii.53)—before there has
been any question of a murder.

There is a conflict, then, between the outward 'strength' of
Beatrice's social position and the wishes and fears that possess her
in secret. But she is presented as her father's daughter, sharing the
imperiousness of the men who are her social equals, and accepting
without question their system of ideas. And as Middleton unfolds
her character in the scenes leading to the play's crisis, the master-
stroke of his portrayal is the way the accepted ideas of her society
become the excuse and even the prompting for her crime. In the
source-story by Reynolds, the 'first plot and designe' of the
murder comes from some 'darke and ambiguous speeches' that
she 'lets fall' to Alsemero.[1] In the play, she utters no more than an
indirect half-wish, and it is Alsemero who translates it into the
thought of a killing, offering her the 'good service' of a challenge
to his rival, as 'The honourablest piece 'bout man, valour'
(II.ii.18–28). Even so, she fails to understand him for a moment,
and then forbids the duel, not because she still hopes to win her
father round, as in the source-story, but out of womanly fear and
prudence:

How? Call you that extinguishing of fear,
When 'tis the only way to keep it flaming? . . .

Beatrice is placed in a similar position to Lady Ager in *A Fair
Quarrel*, who tells her son a lie about her own chastity in order to

---

[1] See Bawcutt, pp. 120–1.

prevent him from fighting a duel. But this time the woman's
arguments have an entirely natural ring:

> Pray, no more, sir.
> Say you prevail'd, y'are danger's and not mine then;
> The law would claim you from me, or obscurity
> Be made the grave to bury you alive. . . .

This is the tenderest speech in the play, the moment where
Beatrice is most appealingly feminine, and comes closest in
sympathy to another human being:

> I'm glad these thoughts come forth; oh keep not one
> Of this condition, sir; here was a course
> Found to bring sorrow on her way to death:
> The tears would ne'er ha' dried, till dust had chok'd 'em . . .

But, with a fine subtlety of portrayal, Middleton makes her hide
her thoughts at the very moment when she is claiming intimacy,
and he makes the turning-point in her speech precisely her
womanly sense of the fitness of things:

> Blood-guiltiness becomes a fouler visage,
> [*Aside*]—And now I think on one: I was to blame,
> I ha' marr'd so good a market with my scorn;
> 'T had been done questionless; the ugliest creature
> Creation fram'd for some use, yet to see
> I could not mark so much where it should be!

Als.　Lady—

Bea.　[*aside*] Why, men of art make much of poison,
　　　　Keep one to expel another; where was my art?

Her thoughts conducing to murder are associated with 'law',
housewifely thrift (the 'market'), the pride of a Jacobean gentle-
woman in her knowledge of cures and simples ('my art') and,
above all, religion and the social order; the fleeting image of a
murderer wandering like Cain melts into the notion of decorum

('becomes') and hardens into the orthodox belief that 'the ugliest creature/ Creation fram'd for some use'. Beatrice justifies her intended use of De Flores to herself exactly as a contemporary like Henry Peacham justifies the privileges of honour, as resulting from 'the Frame of the whole Universe'. In her own eyes, she is hiding her thoughts from her lover in the spirit of a mother deciding what is best for her child. But the dramatic paradox in her asides is that she borrows and identifies herself with Alsemero's proposal of 'valour' and 'service' in the very act of condemning it. The moral contradictions behind the duelling code, already criticized by Middleton and Rowley in *A Fair Quarrel*, here become part and parcel of the heroine's mind.

She has also borrowed from Alsemero the device of removing 'two fears' by a single stroke—in her view, De Flores as well as Alonzo. De Flores alarms her sexually, though she will not admit as much. His 'ugliness' is a brilliant invention by the dramatists— in the original story he had been simply 'a Gallant young Gentleman', 'a fit instrument to execute her will',[1]—since by an implicit black-and-white symbolism (not unlike that used later in *A Game at Chess*) it suggests the perverse fascination he holds for her as well as provoking her hyper-refined recoil. When she thinks of him to replace Alsemero as Alonzo's killer, she designates him, in spite of herself, as her champion, her man. Critics have debated whether her blindness to the price De Flores will demand can be psychologically convincing.[2] But here again Beatrice's social assumptions are important. There is a kind of tidiness, to her mind, in finding a 'use' for him. And, repellent though he is, he fits her purpose because he is a soldier and a 'gentleman'.[3] He can be trusted to combine violence with discretion. At the same time, she cannot imagine that a man so far beneath her in rank, disgraced by his deformity, could dream of touching the lady of the castle, the sought-after bride of some of the 'proudest' gallants in Spain, any more than she can perceive herself as contaminated by the murder she commissions from him. And this assumption would not have

[1] Bawcutt, pp. 122–3.
[2] See Ricks, *art. cit.*, 302.
[3] I.i.134; II.i.48.

seemed astonishing to Jacobean spectators. For example, six years before *The Changeling* was written, after the *cause célèbre* of the Overbury murder—a parallel in some respects to Beatrice's crime —the king had commuted the death sentence on the Countess of Somerset, in view of 'the great and long service of her father, family, and friends', and with the excuse that 'she was not principal but accessory before the fact, and drawn to it by the instigation of base persons'. 'The common people take not this for good payment', Chamberlain had recorded at the time; and Chamberlain had been shocked that Somerset was to be seen in the Tower flaunting 'his garter and George about his neck'—'a man lawfully and publicly convicted of so foul a fact ... But this age affords things as strange and incompatible'.[1] Beatrice's state of mind was no more 'incompatible' with the age. Her compact with De Flores provides a grim comment on contemporary 'honour' and chivalry.

'Payment' and 'service' are key terms in *The Changeling*. In the scenes leading to and following the murder, 'service' is spoken of again and again. Now, it has been pointed out, by Christopher Ricks, that *service* could have a sexual meaning (like a number of other words important in the play); and Ricks has argued that the essential drama turns on these ambiguities. Beatrice fails to see that she cannot have one kind of *service* from De Flores without the other; 'her failure is an egoistic single-mindedness, a tragic failure to see puns'.[2] This may be so, but it is much less than the play conveys. The dramatists are hardly suggesting that had Beatrice only been nimbler-witted, she could have got away with murder. *Service* is ambiguous socially as well as sexually; it can be privileged or lowborn, chivalric or mercenary, rewarded with love or honour or else paid for in cash. And this is the ambiguity that Beatrice plays upon (she is not 'single-minded' here) when she flatters De Flores with

[1] Chamberlain to Carleton, July 20, 1616 (in T. Birch, ed., *The Court and Times of James I*, 1848, I, pp. 419–20); cf. S. R. Gardiner, *History of England, 1603–1642* (1895 edn.), II, p. 361.

[2] Ricks, pp. 296, 302.

> Hardness becomes the visage of a man well,
> It argues service, resolution, manhood,
> If cause were of employment, ...
>
> (II.ii.92)

deceiving him into responding (with a bad faith of his own) by begging for 'the honour of a service', in a gesture of chivalric devotion: 'It's a service that I kneel for to you' (II.ii.96, 117). Each tries to exploit the social duality of the idea, exchanging 'reverence' for a 'precious' 'reward' (II.ii.123, 130).

In the great central scene, the idea of payment is driven home, shattering Beatrice's illusions. In earlier plays, such as *A Chaste Maid in Cheapside* and *A Fair Quarrel*, Middleton had already used commercial metaphors to define ethical values, seriously or ironically. In the latter play, for example, Captain Ager withholds from his duel on the ground that

> he that makes his last peace with his Maker
> In anger, anger is his peace eternally:
> He must expect the same return again
> Whose venture is deceitful;

and the Physician blackmailing Jane after he has sheltered her from disgrace urges her with

> I will tell you, lady, a full quittance,
> And how you may become my creditress ...
> Not in coin, mistress; for silver, though white,
> Yet it draws black lines; it shall not rule my palm
> There to mark forth his base corruption:
> Pay me again in the same quality
> That I to you tendered, – that is, love for love.[1]

De Flores retraces such arguments with a horrifying intensity when Beatrice expects to satisfy him with money:

> Do you place me in the rank of verminous fellows,
> To destroy things for wages? Offer gold?

[1] III. i (ed. Havelock Ellis, Mermaid edn., II, p. 240), III. ii (p. 247).

> The life blood of man! Is anything
> Valued too precious for my recompense?
>
> (III.iv.64)

There is devastating irony in his own choice of metaphor:

> I could ha' hir'd
> A journeyman in murder at this rate,
> And mine own conscience might have slept at ease
> And have had the work brought home.

For all the word-play of chivalry between them earlier, this represents precisely what Beatrice had wanted to do. It is she who has been 'forgetful', he says (94, 96); and in his passionate plea, 'Justice invites your blood to understand me' (100), besides the sexual vehemence there is the shock of an unmanageable truth. It is as if indeed her virginity was the only possible 'recompense' for 'the life blood of man'. Their dialogue pursues relentlessly the logic involved in this primitive equation:

> *Bea.* Think but upon the distance that creation
> Set 'twixt thy blood and mine, and keep thee there.
>
> *De F.* Look but into your conscience, read me there,
> 'Tis a true book, you'll find me there your equal . . .
>
> (III.iv.130)

For the moment, he speaks as a radical Puritan, and his 'true book' is surely a book of accounts. His metaphors from the 'market' sweep aside her supposed absolutes of 'blood', 'birth' and 'parentage'.

Every word in this dialogue sparkles with irony. Beatrice has 'chang'd', as he reminds her (143). As Antonio's rôle in the sub-plot brings out, a *changeling* was a fool or half-wit. But it also meant a turncoat, a renegade to nobility. In *The Nobles* (1563), for example, Laurence Humphrey writes that 'Commonly the childe expresseth his sire, and posterity (if not chaungeling) covets to tread the steps of their auncestours', and that noblemen, 'if not chaungelynges, encrease the praises of their auncestours with theyr owne prowesse'; and Shakespeare uses the word similarly when he makes Henry IV describe the Percies' followers as 'fickle changelings', or makes Aufidius declare that Coriolanus is 'no changeling' in pride, even though he has deserted from Rome to the Volscians.[1] It is a changeling status, in both senses, that De Flores fastens on Beatrice:

> Y'are the deed's creature; by that name
> You lost your first condition, and I challenge you,
> As peace and innocency has turn'd you out,
> And made you one with me.
>
> (III.iv.137)

'I challenge': he lays claim to her[2]—as someone might claim the legal guardianship of a changeling, or fool. At the same time, his lines recall her own latently biblical image when she feared to think of Alsemero as a homeless outlaw. From this point forward, the whole movement of the play shows Beatrice's myth of 'creation' recoiling upon herself.

Apart from *Women Beware Women* (which may however have been the later of Middleton's two masterpieces), there is nothing in earlier Jacobean drama to compare with *The Changeling* for its penetrating analysis of a social myth. Clearly, Beatrice might have been, but is not, presented as an example of the 'insolencie' of women. Nor is she, essentially, the victim of contemporary marriage arrangements, though Isabella's rôle in the sub-plot helps to give a certain force to this consideration in the play. Beatrice makes her own hell; but she does so with the unconscious complicity of the men of her own rank around her, by blindly trusting in their prejudices and beliefs. Her mind is a mirror of social certitudes. Webster's Duchess of Malfi, whose tragedy

---

[1] *The Nobles* (1563), c. i^v, k. i. 4^v; *1 Henry IV*, v.i.76, and *Coriolanus*, IV. vii. 11. (For a similar use much later, see the farmer's letter in Godwin's *Caleb Williams*, II., ch. 2 (1794: ed. Herbert van Thal, 1966, p. 124): 'if we little folks had but the wit to do for ourselves, the great folks would not be such maggotty changelings as they are'.)

[2] Cf. *The Witch of Edmonton*, I.ii.209 (ed. R. G. Lawrence, in *Jacobean and Caroline Comedies*, 1973).

Middleton and Rowley copied from and admired, had chosen a husband of lower rank virtuously or at least pardonably, but with the clear knowledge that she was defying the world. Beatrice plunges into the crime that makes her De Flores' partner in an unquestioning confidence that her world must be on her side.

At the same time, the thoroughness with which Beatrice's mind is dissected limits the total impact of the play; not that the playwrights are detached, but that they are too sternly engaged. Her fate, pathetic as it is, comes across in the end rather as a terrible demonstration of moral law than as an emotionally painful if unavoidable loss. And none of the other characters counteract this effect, or broaden its imaginative range. De Flores is as probable and poetical as Leigh Hunt declared, a cynical underdog obsessed by an impossible desire; but though he recalls philosophizing malcontents in the tradition of Iago or Bosola, the dramatists resolutely confine his rôle. The sub-plot is widely defended today as an extension of the main themes in the play, and by no means an excrescence. But no one could claim that it has much interest in itself, and it seems only too plainly inserted for the sake of thematic counterpoint. Tomazo's part can also be defended, since it is used to show that Beatrice and De Flores are destroyed by their own actions and not by a conventional revenger. The last speeches in the play dwell on justice and reconciliation. But dramatically they are too humane, since Alsemero becomes a dispassionate judge instead of an anguished husband. And his rôle after the first scenes has been restrained and unemotional, apparently with this object in view. The dramatists, in short, are more concerned by the end with justice than with tragedy. This comes near to what one critic means by accusing them of a 'failure of nerve'; yet it is unfair on that account to charge them with making deliberate 'concessions to the taste of the time'.[1] On the contrary, they seem too thoroughly committed to criticism. In the late Jacobean theatres, only a Shakespeare perhaps could have transcended such a purpose and found subject for tragic celebration in his characters while at the same time dissecting their social morality so searchingly.

[1] G. R. Hibbard, 'The Tragedies of Thomas Middleton and the Decadence of the Drama', *Renaissance and Modern Studies* I (U. of Nottingham, 1957).

VII

Myth and Victorian Melodrama

KURT TETZELI von ROSADOR

I

MYTH criticism belongs to those approaches to literature which produce the predictable reaction of which a mockingly raised eyebrow is the external sign and critical neglect—far from being benign—the inevitable consequence. No doubt, there are a number of good reasons why this is so. Foremost among these reasons is the rigid dogmatism with which mythologists have pursued their studies in the past, imposing unity on discrepant and diffuse material, frequently on the flimsiest of evidence. Thus all-inclusive theory after all-inclusive theory has been apodictically promoted. Yet Max Müller's omnipotent and omnipresent solar deity had to relinquish its reign after all, to be closely followed by Frazer's dying god. And still the Jungian shadow looms large. Equal damage to the cause of myth criticism was done by the extravagant, high claims for its aims and results. Holding as a dogma that literature is nothing but a variation, a reworking, a displacement of an original myth or myths, myth criticism tends to confine itself to the unravelling of this basic mythical pattern. Then its goal is reached, the work is explained. Aesthetic consider-ations do not unduly concern this myth critic. All extant literature shrinks to a variation on a (mythic) theme, reductionism has its field-day, and the golden bough is used as the master-key to unlock the secrets of all literature. Literary value is accorded proportionately to the amount of mythical themes used—the more the better.[1]

---

[1] *Cf.* Philip Rahv's onslaught on this premise implicit in much myth criticism in his *The Myth and the Powerhouse* (New York, 1965), p. 21.

Yet although excesses may lay bare inherent weaknesses of the method—they certainly do lay bare those of its proponents—it would be quite wrong to deny myth criticism its use and its place among the approaches to literature. At the most basic level, single myths and whole mythologies have served as raw material, as source matter for literature through the ages. The insistence with which myths have been consciously revived over and over again in all genres of literature and with which they have functioned as vehicles for the literature of different times and different places proves the close affinity which exists between those two creations of man. As documents in the natural history of the human mind, analogously structured and serving analogous needs, they can be—on another level—usefully and meaningfully compared. To do this there is no need to join the raging controversy over the definition of myth. The analogy can be drawn without deciding whether myth precedes ritual or whether it is 'a narrative linked with a rite' (Lord Raglan), 'the depersonalized dream' (Joseph Campbell), a 'collective fantasy embodying ideals and memories' (Harry Levin), or whether myths are simply 'stories that have become traditional' (Stith Thompson).[1]

To utilize myth for the study of literature, the common denominator in these definitions is of greater importance than the quite obvious differences, extensive as they may be. Almost universally acknowledged among myth critics is the assumption that 'the creating of myths, the mythopoeic faculty, is inherent in the thinking process'.[2] It follows that mythic patterns are bound both to be near-universal and to recur through the ages. The universality and historical priority of myth leads the stricter myth critics to conclude that 'myth forms the matrix out of which literature emerges both historically and psychologically'.[3] Yet there is no logical necessity for this conclusion. Granted that the myth-making faculty is inherent in the thinking process and that

[1] Two essay collections, edited by Thomas A. Sebeok, *Myth. A Symposium* (Bloomington–London, 1958) and Henry A. Murray, *Myth and Mythmaking* (New York, 1960), provide succinct statements of the various views.

[2] John B. Vickery, 'Introduction' to *Myth and Literature: Contemporary Theory and Practice* (Lincoln, Nebr., 1966), p. ix.

[3] *Ibid.*

myth enjoys historical priority, this does not mean that literature is merely myth in disguise. It only means that the making of myth and the making of literature are closely related processes and that the patterns, themes, figures, situations, plots, of myth are *likely* to be also the stuff of literature. The very essence or structure of literature can therefore never be illuminated by describing its hidden or overt mythic contents. What the disclosure of near-universal and recurrent mythic patterns in works of literature can do is to explain the emotional hold the work has on us. The universality and recurrence of mythic patterns are conclusive and emphatic proof of their appeal to our basic emotional needs, and this appeal is exerted regardless of any literary merit. Where myth criticism rightly belongs is therefore neither in the definition nor in the evaluation of the work of art. What it can legitimately do is provide plausible reasons for our reactions to it.

Yet in analysing myths and literature one must be alert to the fact that different procedures are needed. Close reading is only partly applicable to the study of myth. In discovering the mythic contents in literature one has to take into account that—as Claude Lévi-Strauss has forcefully and persuasively pointed out—'a myth is still felt as a myth by any reader throughout the world. Its substance does not lie in its style, its original music, or its syntax, but in the *story* which it tells'.[1] It is the movement of the plot, the situation itself, the constellation of the figures which more often than not convey the mythic content and evoke its powerful associations. Through an analysis of story line or situational effects most submerged myths can be discovered. Language and imagery take second place as analytic tools. Only those myths which consist mainly in projecting a mood or in the unfolding of a static, picturelike situation rely also on linguistic subtleties, on image-clusters and the pregnant metaphor, for their adequate portrayal. An investigation of Victorian melodrama can supply ample proof of this. In my interpretation of melodrama's mythic content I shall give examples for both, the myth latent in and structured by the movement of the action and the myth mainly expressed through verbal allusions and metaphors.

[1] 'The Structural Study of Myth', in: Sebeok, *op. cit.*, pp. 85 f.

II

The strong emotional appeal and powerful effect of Victorian melodrama has been variously discussed. In his influential study Michael Booth, for example, has richly enumerated the causes for the amazing and enduring popularity of melodrama.[1] Prominent among these causes is the easy and clear-cut morality propounded in the plays, a morality executed through the most rigid poetic justice—hardly anything else but a barely humanized form of the *lex talionis*. Thus the spectator was not unduly troubled intellectually, but was allowed both to suffer with the hero by identifying with him and to right the evils of the world by ridding himself of all his aggression at the expense of the villain. Moreover, the fixed personnel of melodrama, the stereotyped *dramatis personae*, acting out over and over again an extremely limited number of dramatic patterns, like those of flight and pursuit, intrigue and victimization, certainly made for easy consumption. And, to name one last reason for its astounding Victorian career, melodrama served unashamedly an escapist function, portraying realms of wish fulfilment, a function of which playwrights and critics were frequently aware.

All this may be considered sufficient explanation for the immense attraction melodrama had for its audiences. Still, some doubt lingers whether something as one-dimensional and superficial, as repetitive and stereotyped, as melodrama is deemed to be, could have enthralled audiences for almost a century, audiences which contained all the layers of society—from Queen Victoria herself to rowdy members of the industrial proletariat. A genre which manages to appeal to the tastes, interests and needs of audiences so unlike and diverse could hardly have done this merely by the endless dramatization of a few quite simple patterns. Even if the brilliant scenic inventions and sensational effects of Victorian melodrama are also taken into account, there remains the fact that no other dramatic genre of such avowed simplicity has ever ruled the boards and taken in so large an audience for so long a time.

[1] *English Melodrama* (London, 1965), espec. p. 187.

It is the thesis of this essay that submerged mythic themes have contributed not inconsiderably to this phenomenal success. Obviously, no extensive documentation of mythic themes can be attempted here. I shall restrict myself to pointing out a few occurrences of submerged myths or mythic patterns. I shall then attempt a somewhat fuller analysis of the one myth which I consider to be basic to melodrama and melodramatic thinking, the myth of the golden age.

III

Although Victorian melodrama has only very rarely dealt directly with gods and goddesses, mythic heroes and heroines, other genres of Victorian drama have not similarly abstained. Throughout the nineteenth century, and more especially from the 1850s onwards, Greek mythology was ridiculed. Medea, Ixion, Orpheus, Antigone, Prometheus and even Pentheus were sometimes vigorously, more often outrageously, burlesqued. As burlesque only prospers if the audience has at least some smattering of its matter, it presupposes some basic knowledge of and interest in mythology in its audience, an interest which itself seems to have been parodied. What else can the title of a burlesque like *Mythology Run Mad* (1893) mean? (Unfortunately, no copy of the play by Theodore Moore and E. Runtz has survived.) This interest was subliminally fed by frequent dramatizations of mythic or mythlike themes and figures. Vampires[1] (among other ghosts and ghouls) people the Victorian melodramatic stage. Both Ondine and Loreley wove their spells of enchantment and fatal attraction there. The Flying Dutchman and the Wandering Jew crisscrossed the boards of the minor houses throughout the century, entirely in keeping with their fateful curse. All these figures, of course, did not originate with melodrama, but were borrowed or adapted or

---

[1] *Cf.* the dramatic pedigree given by A. Owen Aldrige, 'The Vampire Theme: Dumas Père and the English Stage', in *Expression, Communication and Experience in Literature and Language*, ed. Ronald G. Popperwell (London, 1973), pp. 285–6.

stolen from authors like Lord Byron, Dumas père or Eugène Sue, writers much more myth-conscious than the average melodramatist. Still, this does not reduce the mythic aura these figures possess within their respective melodramas. Their being used also in melodrama rather is a powerful indication of their profound emotional appeal and of melodrama's adequacy as a vehicle for mythic themes.

No wonder, then, that mythic themes are ubiquitous in melodrama. The perpetual struggle between good and evil Northrop Frye has described as the central form of romance which, in Frye's terminology, is myth displaced 'in a human direction'.[1] Both myth and romance are certainly products of man's mythopoeic faculty. As is well known, this conflict of good and evil is also the hallmark of melodrama: hero and villain are the combatants, and cosmic forces are involved. The mythic dimension of this conflict is probably best shown in J. B. Buckstone's *The Ice Witch; or, The Frozen Hand* (1831). At the most fundamental level of the plot Druda, the Ice Witch, and Freyr, the Sun God, compete for sovereignty. While Druda manages to enthral the hero Harold, who is 'Odin's lineal offspring' (I.1), for a brief, wintry spell, the Sun God, love, and new life triumph predictably in the end. Freyr explains the cyclical movement of the plot: 'Winter hath passed away, and Summer reigns in triumph' (II.4). It seems clear that more is involved here than the mere conflict of good and evil. As Mircea Eliade has shown in a brilliant book,[2] the battle of summer and winter, manifested in the endless cycle of the seasons, the revolution of the planets and the rising and setting sun are central to the myth of the eternal return, of which Buckstone's melodrama is thus a direct representation. Moreover, the movement of the sun, with its daily death and daily rise, belongs inextricably to another well-known and highly influential myth, that of the dying god. That this mythic range of Buckstone's play is not a modern supersubtle interpretation can be shown by the 'Remarks' which George Daniel, one of the most perceptive of critics of early-Victorian popular drama, has pre-

[1] *Anatomy of Criticism* (Princeton, 1957), p. 137.
[2] *Le Mythe de l'éternel retour* (Paris, 1949).

fixed to the acting version of the play. Staged on Easter Monday—
the time of another annual resurrection—*The Ice Witch* according
to Daniel is fit for 'this joyous saturnalia'. Time and theme
cohere, and the Victorian critic is aware of the aptness of the
relationship.

Although Buckstone's *The Ice Witch* is outstanding in its rich-
ness of mythic contents, it is in no ways singular among Victorian
melodramas.[1] The cosmic dimension of the conflict of good and
evil can be paralleled in plays like W. T. Moncrieff's *The Vampire*
(1830), where the eponymous villain is opposed by the goddesses
Terra and Lunaria, while in Fitzball's version of *The Flying
Dutchman* (1830) Vanderdecken's real antagonist is the god of
winds, Aeolus. Of equal importance for a good many plots of
Victorian melodrama is the myth of the dying god. In Henry
Arthur Jones' *The Silver King* (1882) good and typical use is made
of this myth. It is first alluded to and then acted out, when the
train accident provides Wilfred Denver with the chance of a new
beginning in life. 'Wilfred Denver is dead!' exclaims the hero,
'To-morrow I begin a new life!' (II.4). Thus, to his family and the
world Denver dies; he assumes another name, returns a rich
man, but resumes his identity only when he is being cleansed
of the crime his old self had been accused of: 'I'm your father
that was dead—I am alive again and I have come home to you'
(V.2).

As has been frequently remarked, this plot-scheme, the seeming
death, the surprise return, the quasi-resurrection, belongs to the
stock-in-trade of melodrama. Its occurrences can hardly be
numbered. If plays as widely divergent in date, setting, and atmosphere as Milner's *Mazeppa* (1831), Haines' *My Poll and My
Partner Joe* (1835), Hazlewood's *Lady Audley's Secret* (1863), and
Jones' *The Silver King* (1882)[2] incorporate identical structural and
thematic elements, the suggestion that more is involved than the

[1] Here and elsewhere I am using the term Victorian to comprehend all
nineteenth-century melodrama. The consistency of the genre, of its structural and
thematic features, throughout the century can serve as a justification for this
usage.

[2] To which can be added H. O. Anderton's lyrical drama *Baldur* (London,
1893), representing one of the 'classical' versions of the myth of the dying god.

mere repetition of a box-office proven formula seems not too far-fetched. What is additionally involved is the opposition, the battle between life and death, in which ultimately life always triumphs. As Mazeppa rhetorically puts it: 'Have I then passed the realm of death? And do I wake to new life and other being?' (II.6). For the heroes of melodrama death is a transitory stage, to be passed unharmed. After monstrous dangers and seeming death the hero is regularly rewarded with life, not to mention love and fortune. The plot-scheme, reworking the myth of the dying god, affirms in each case the triumphant renewal of life. Thus it lies at the very heart of the genre, giving shape to melodrama's presupposition of an eternally fixed, unshakeable, and harmonious world-order, to the presentation of which, it may be said, all themes and dramatic techniques are subservient.

Furthermore, this variant of the myth of the dying god is but one version of the hero's career in melodrama. In a good number of plays, in Milner's *Mazeppa*, Fitzball's *Thalaba* (1822) and Taylor's *The Serf* (1865), to name but three, the hero's life is closely patterned on the recognized mythic prototype.[1] All these three plays could have served Lord Raglan as textbooks for drafting the hero's typical biography had he known them.[2] They make use of all or (as in the case of *The Serf*) of most of the following typical plot-elements which are invariably presented in fixed sequence: The child comes from royal or noble stock; perils surround its birth; it is spirited away, handed over to foster-parents and brought up by them in a distant country; the child-hood is not presented; on reaching manhood he enters on the quest to regain identity and his hereditary fortune; he undergoes extreme dangers, such as travelling through the underworld or passing the realm of death; he kills a monster, human or other-wise; through this he achieves his destined and rightful position and marries. In the glory of this happy state the plays end.

[1] That the first two plays take over their structure from Southey and Byron respectively does not lessen their claim to mythic relevance. On the contrary, the choice of material is proof of melodrama's and the melodramatists' affinity and inclination towards myth.

[2] Lord Raglan, *The Hero. A Study in Tradition, Myth, and Drama* (London, 1936), pp. 179–80.

Abstracted, the movement from a harmonious state through danger and disorder to renewed bliss constitutes the course of all melodrama,[1] a course which the career of the hero reflects and which then is expressive of the same harmonious world-order as the reworking of the myth of the dying god.

There is certainly no lack of other mythic patterns integrated into melodrama. M. W. Disher, for example, has devoted his cursory study of melodrama mainly to the concept of maiden purity and its plentiful dramatic manifestations. As the material assembled there will reveal its mythic analogues and dimensions without difficulty, I feel absolved from going over it here.[2] Instead let me briefly draw attention to another myth submerged in the plot-structure of melodrama, a myth of almost equal importance as that of the hero's life and the dying god and not totally unrelated to either. As melodrama's initial blissful state of being disintegrates, as disorder rears its ugly head, the evil thus come into existence must be righted if harmony is to be established again. One highly effective way of doing just this is through loading one of the figures with all the guilt, all the sins of the community. Then the sin-laden figure is driven out and killed. It is effected, in short, through the scapegoat: in a trice, by the casting out and/or annihilation of the scapegoat, all evil is removed, the community completely purified and full harmony established.

The use melodrama makes of this emotionally powerful—powerful because mythically given—motif is quite complex and would deserve further extensive study. No doubt, it is the villain who is cast most regularly in the rôle of the scapegoat. He personifies all evil, he is the one misfit in an otherwise well-ordered dramatic universe. His removal removes the one threat to the well-being of the community. More interesting is the case of

---

[1] In a few melodramas (e.g. John Walker's *The Factory Lad* or Douglas Jerrold's *Fifteen Years of a Drunkard's Life*) this plot-scheme is inverted to the steady downward course of the hero, the progressive disintegration of order, serving a hortatory function.

[2] *Cf.* his *Melodrama. Plots That Thrilled* (London, 1954). Although Disher does not explicitly deal with the mythic dimension of this concept, he is aware of melodrama's 'cosmic partiality for the virginal' (p. XIII).

those plays in which the guilt is shifted to (seemingly) respectable characters. In Haines' *The Wizard of the Wave* (1840) it is Don José, the father of the heroine, who bewails his fate in the following manner: 'Eternal fiends! why, why am I pursued? From earliest youth, ruin and disappointment still have dogged my footsteps; thwarted in wealth—in love—ambition—everything! When triumph seemed within my grasp, ruin has dashed the dream away!' (II.2) Though having sinned in the past, all that Don José does in the play is to put obstacles in the way of true love. This is the truly melodramatic cause of Don José's ruin. The real villainy in Haines' play is committed by melodrama's appropriate personage. Here, the rôles of villain and scapegoat are split; the spectator is allowed the luxury of pitying the victim of society's needs—for what else is, in the last analysis, a scapegoat?[1]—while being able to lay all blame for this action on the villain.

Even more interesting is the figure of the scapegoat in plays in which the hero seems to be destined to act out this part, in which he is—to quote the subtitle of Joseph Lunn's *The Shepherd of Derwent Vale* (1825)—'The Innocent Culprit'. Misdeed after misdeed is then ascribed to him: 'I am a MURDERER!' cries the desperate Alvanley, the seducer of the heroine in Moncrieff's *The Lear of Private Life* (1828), who will yet make her honest in the end, 'a double murderer! Traitor to Love and Nature! outcast of Heaven and man!' (II.4) The scapegoat hero sinks into misery, and everybody turns from him, as society inexorably demands its due, his sacrifice. 'Expose her! Expel her from society in which she is an intruder!', screams outraged society's personification in Augustin Daly's *Under the Gaslight* (1867). Or else turns silently away to exclude the hero as effectively as in Tom Taylor's *The Ticket-of-Leave Man* (IV.1). But, of course, the hero culprit is really innocent. His guilt vanishes as merely imaginary and is laid where it belongs, at the feet of the villain, or else his real worth is proven by an act

[1] Douglas Jerrold, most socially conscious of early-Victorian popular playwrights, points to this in his *Fifteen Years of a Drunkard's Life* (1828): 'If a man once fall', comments one of the characters, a miserable drunkard himself, 'no matter when—no matter how he may have suffered—repented of the rashness—the good, respectable people of this world, raise their hands, set up the long loud cry' (III. 2).

of social value (as is the case in *The Lear of Private Life*). The emotional power of this figure and plot-structure can hardly be overestimated. It allows the spectator to have the cake and eat it, to take downright pleasure in the sufferings and persecutions the hero has to undergo, because he knows quite well that both the end of the mythic pattern, the purification of society, will be achieved and that the hero's suffering is transitory and serves this higher end. The emotional power of the myth is invoked, without paying the mythic price. Small wonder then, that melodrama has so often been deprecatingly called pseudotragedy.

IV

So far I have merely sketched a number of mythic patterns and their submerged versions in the plot-structures of melodrama. I have restricted myself to a rather cursory treatment because I hope that, once pointed to, the existence of so widely known mythic patterns may become obvious and because I know that detailed exposition and cumulative argumentation in the face of melo-drama's simple and transparent structures must prove tedious. In the following I shall try to show the importance of still another myth to melodrama's impressive emotional power, the myth of the golden age. This myth can only partly be embodied in the plot. It must be depicted through scenery and imagery. Therefore, it needs must be presented in this essay in closer detail, using quotations where earlier on a short outline of the plot was sufficient. The nature of the myth itself necessitates this approach. It is in origin a composite myth, comprising divergent material and possessing, as it were, an additive, a cumulative structure. As Harry Levin has pointed out in his rich and illuminating study this myth, contrary to those dealt with so far, has no one protagon-ist, no definite plot-structure or iconology, 'because the concept [of the golden age] is so general; rather than tell a story, it pro-jects a mood'.[1] To project a mood the dramatist has to rely on

---

[1] *The Myth of the Golden Age in the Renaissance* (London, 1970), p. 113. I am much indebted to Levin's study.

other means than extensive action or close-knitted plot. Evocative, not narrative, techniques will therefore predominate in its presentation.

There is no need to trace the origins of the myth or to describe fully its essence—Harry Levin has done that for us. It will be enough for our purposes to list the elements of which the myth consists. At its heart lies man's yet unstilled desire for an ideally harmonious world. Thus the myth is oriented in time to both the beginning and the end of the world and the widespread assumptions about them, the paradisian garden and the millennial state. The central quality, attributed to these harmonious and perfect states, is pleasure, a life of total and unabashed pleasure in the idyllic surroundings of a *locus amoenus*. Closely related to this *topos* is the reality and the imagery of the garden and the country, of Arcadia. There permanent spring reigns, only the month of May fits the beauty of this green world. Perfect and young love falls to the human lot. It seems hardly surprising that melodrama has made such consistent use of these elements. The pleasure principle, the hankering after the perfect harmony, is the main motive force behind the myth of the golden age. And it is the pleasure principle, too, which dominates the world of Victorian melodrama.

Often the rise of the curtain allows the spectator a first glance at a Victorian variety of the *locus amoenus*. An idyllic landscape, a rural setting, is the scenic prospect for the opening of a good many melodrama: 'A Village Green—Country Church in the distance. In the centre of the stage stands a May-pole.' This stage-direction from Buckstone's *The May Queen* (1834) can be taken as a typical example. Flowers and trees,[1] neat little houses and a neat little church concretize this Victorian and domestic version of the pleasant place. As a matter of course, it is springtime, the season for May-games and merrymaking. The mere setting oozes perfect harmony. The opening of James M'Closkey's *The Fatal Glass; or,*

[1] In a different context Peter Brooks in his ingenious study, *The Melodramatic Imagination. Balzac, Henry James, Melodrama, and the Mode of Excess* (New Haven—London, 1976), p. 29, has noted the prevalence of the garden setting in melodrama.

The Curse of Drink (1872) provides a more extensive and graphic example and adds further elements of the myth:

> Village landscape, with mill at back, LUE, at work.—Set water.—Bridge across back.—Set house, R2E covered with trellis and flowers.—Garden chairs, RC.—Bank, C.—Lights up at opening.—Mill heard at work.

> Enter Villagers, at rise of curtain, across bridge, with flowers, festoons, etc., singing rural music. Villagers sing—

> > Mabel Grey, your friends have come
> > To wish you joy upon this day;
> > You give your hand to him you love,
> > In this blooming, flowery month of May.

The scenery conjures up an idyllic, pastoral atmosphere. Of course, it is spring and the month of May, too. Moreover, it is a day of high festivity, of young love fulfilled. No wonder, the bridegroom thinks the golden age at hand when he hears the peals of the marriage bells: 'Oh, Mabel! how my heart beats in response to those joyous moments! They proclaim a new existence to me; a heaven upon earth! its portals open, I see beyond a garden teeming with golden fruit' (1.1). Here the mythic analogue is expressly evoked. Yet even without the explicit reference, the scenery and the song depict the main elements of the myth, the idyllic landscape, the springtime atmosphere, the feasting, merry-making, and unrestrained young love. An opening chorus, too, is frequently employed in melodrama for this purpose. In C. Z. Barnett's *The Dream of Fate* (1838) it is again sung in jubilant celebration of a wedding. And Henry Holl's *Grace Huntley* (1833) adjures in a drinking song 'old Time without end', the timeless bliss of the golden age.

All these examples serve identical functions. They establish the atmosphere of the play by providing with the very first scene the foil against which the events to follow are set. They demonstrate that the perfect life, that ideal harmony, does exist in this day and age. The mythically charged material guarantees the playwright the intended effect. Melodrama thus commences by drawing a picture of a happy and timeless existence, a Victorian picture of the golden age. But this myth of the golden age, unlike those of the hero, the dying god, the scapegoat, is not dramatic in itself. Furthermore, its presentation in the first scene is a postulate, a *donnée*, the value and stability of which have to be dramatically tested. To dramatize and to prove the myth, the melodramatist 'hath the serpent brought'. Evil in the person of the villain at once enters the paradisian garden. The mythic analogy is, appropriately enough, extended to the villain by likening him to the arch-tempter, the serpent in Eden. Thus, outspoken villainy gloats in the accepted melodramatic manner in Haines' *The Wizard of the Wave*: 'So now for the bower of innocence—the serpent's tongue in Eden was not more musical when he turned tempter than mine shall be' (I.I).

With the attack of evil on the harmonious idyll the relevance, even the existence of the mythic golden age, are at stake. All through melodrama villainy appears to triumph, the life and virtue of the hero and heroine are jeopardized, the golden age seems irredeemably to recede and to fade out of existence. Yet closer study demonstrates that the playwrights keep the idea of the golden age steadfastly alive. A variety of techniques is employed to achieve this purpose. Simple description of its continued existence assures the spectator that the mythic golden conditions can bear the brunt of the attacks of the wicked: 'Look round you and by the brilliant light of the bright and glorious sun, note the beauty of the world that heaven has given its creatures. Look on yon limpid stream, flowing like molten silver to the sea. Look on the trees—the hills—the vallies—all made exquisite by providence divine. Gaze on the wondrous work of matchless excellence and loveliness' (II.4).[1] But if the golden age continues to exist unharmed despite the eruption of evil in its midst, the power of evil is implicitly belittled; its forceful clash with good, on which melodrama thrives, dwindles to an unequally balanced squabble. No true melodramatist will so easily forego the thrills and shudders the might of evil can provoke. On

[1] Samuel Atkyns, *The Wandering Jew; or, The Veteran, the Brute-Tamer, and the Orphan Girls*, B.M. Add. MS 42978.

the contrary, he will exaggerate the powers of villainy and then frustrate them. Thus, a more dramatically adequate means to keep the spectator aware of the possibility of a golden age is to remind him of its past splendour: 'Ay, those were gay days! Then, life seemed full of promise, as a field of ripened corn. Those were happy times!' (1.3), muses old Martin in Jerrold's *The Rent-Day* (1832). And his nostalgic backward look is complemented by the assurance that the happy times will recur again: 'They will come back; never fear it', is the answer Martin receives. For this optimistic outlook melodrama can advance good proof. The certainty of belief the *dramatis personae* express in the reestablishment of the harmonious, idyllic state is based on the firm trust in the workings of a providential destiny: 'We shall have better days yet. He who tempers the wind to the shorn lamb will not suffer us to sink' (1.1).[1] The workings of providence ensure the promised outcome; they are firmly oriented towards the realization of a (domesticated) millennial state, a state in which evil is cast out and clinically pure good victorious. Through maxim after maxim, the spectator is told that providence exists and will not suffer the wicked to triumph, for 'when the clouds are thickest, the sun still shines behind them' (IV.1).[2]

Despite the villain's perfidious machinations, despite the seemingly irretrievable loss of the Arcadian state of innocence and bliss, the audience can therefore entertain no reasonable doubt about the glory ahead. Poetic justice will be meted out and the golden age restored. Accordingly, evil—in spite of its power and pervasiveness—is reduced to an instrumental function in the plans of destiny. Analogous to its function in Christian theodicy it is employed for bringing about final harmony. The melodramatist and his audience were fully conscious that 'out of evil cometh good',[3] to quote the appropriate maxim which also served C. H. Stephenson as a title for a melodrama. If evil was permitted to flaunt its powers, it was 'for wise purposes' only.[4] And the

---

[1] W. Thompson Townsend, *Old Adam* (1853).
[2] Tom Taylor, *The Ticket-of-Leave Man* (1863).
[3] J. B. Buckstone, *The Dream at Sea* (1835), III. 1.
[4] J. R. Planché, *The Vampire* (1820), 'Introductory Vision'.

wise purposes of providence ensured the spectator that a state equivalent to the paradisian garden and the golden age was to be revealed at the play's close.

To bring about this final blissful and golden state melodrama consistently preferred two means. One of them has already been discussed: the casting out of the scapegoat rids the dramatic cosmos of all evil. The purification of society thus effected can also be achieved by an even more spectacular theatrical means, namely, the apocalyptic destruction of the old rotten order, out of the ruins of which the innocent and happy new world may arise. In this the myth of the golden age reveals its utopian and millennial tendencies. As the millennium is traditionally introduced by wholesale destruction, so melodrama's penultimate scene is fairly regularly one of cataclysmic catastrophe. From Pocock's *The Miller and His Men* to the sensational melodramas of 'Druriolanus' Harris the reestablishment of order and the apotheosis of young love is preceded by the violent destruction of the tainted old world. Floods and fires—the natural forces so common to all millennial myths—are the much used means to this end.[1] Their mythic powers of purification combine with the thrills of spectacular stage-effects to make this scene one of the main attractions of Victorian melodrama (a view which is borne out by the century-long admiration of the gaping theatre-crowd for this type of scene).

Then peace and harmony reign again. Poetic justice guarantees that only the good survive and that they will live happily after: 'Yes, years in happiness are in store for us all'.[2] The presentation of the golden age at the conclusion of melodrama relies on much the same methods as at its first exposition. To give just one example from Leopold Lewis' version of *The Wandering Jew*

---

[1] Already George Daniel was provoked to comment punningly apropos *The Miller and His Men*: 'When language fails, and invention is at a stand, what fills up the awkward interval with such effect as a flash—("O for a muse of *fire!*") not of wit, but of gunpowder?—A piece with an explosion is sure to go off well", *Cumberland's British Theatre*, 26 (n.d.), pp. 5 f. Political symbolism for the selfsame explosion is claimed by Irena Dobrzycka, 'English Nineteenth Century Melodrama: Themes and Techniques', *Kwartalnik neofilologiczny*, 22 (1975), p. 399.

[2] William W. Pratt, *Ten Nights in a Bar-Room* (1858), v. 3.

(1873).[1] Here the *locus amoenus* is again scenically realized: 'The back of scene rises and sinks discovering the dawn of day, a beautiful landscape.' The break of day, the rising sun, the season of spring are evoked over and over again.[2] They stress the youth, the freshness, and innocence of the final and unalterable achievement. But it is the Victorian version of total pleasure, the domestic bliss of married love, which crowns all. As hero and heroine embrace place, time, and human fate cohere. And on this tableau of ideal love in an ideal environment the falling curtain closes.

V

The dramatic technique of presenting myth in melodrama deserves a final word or two. The examples given should have made clear that no Victorian melodramatist ventured consciously on the revival of myth. Myth survived unconsciously in the drama (as in the novel). No extensive treatment can, therefore, be expected. Just as the Victorian system of values is incorporated into melodrama by the mere mention of emotionally strategic words like home, family, children, work, duty, nice and neat, the mythic material is integrated into plot, theme, *dramatis personae*, and imagery in an allusive manner, in dramatic shorthand, as it were. Melodrama derives its power not from mythic patterns clearly to be discerned by the audience, but from evocative analogies which do their work subliminally and from the potency of the myths preferred. The myths of the scapegoat and of the golden age may be singled out because of their particular aptness for the genre.

It may be objected—and this is an objection with which all myth criticism has been repeatedly confronted—that myths can be discovered in all drama, if such a pattern as that from harmony through chaos to harmony claims mythic relevance. Then—runs

---

[1] B.M. Add. MS 53121C.

[2] *Cf.* the final words of the hero of *London by Night*: 'Your existence hitherto has been a long night, but there is a morning. Let us hope that it will bring sunlight, genial gales, and comfort to your future days.'

the objection—all fish will be caught in such a wide net. True, but with that controversy this essay has not been concerned. It has been concerned with analysing one historically circumscribed literary phenomenon, the Victorian melodrama, and with establishing that certain concrete myths, especially that of the golden age, structured it. This analysis has been undertaken on the presupposition that myths submerged in literary texts cannot be used to ascribe aesthetic value to such works. Yet the recurrence and universality of these myths appears to be powerful proof of their persistent and strong emotional appeal. This analysis can therefore serve to explain, or rather to contribute to the explanation of, the longevity of such an apparently simplistic dramatic formula, as that of the melodramatic genre is widely held to be.